P9-DXK-966

ISLAM BEYOND THE VIOLENT JIHADIS

PROVOCATIONS

ISLAM BEYOND THE VIOLENT JIHADIS
AN OPTIMISTIC MUSLIM SPEAKS

ZIAUDDIN SARDAR

SERIES EDITOR:
YASMIN ALIBHAI-BROWN

Biteback Publishing

First published in Great Britain in 2016 by
Biteback Publishing Ltd
Westminster Tower
3 Albert Embankment
London SE1 7SP
Copyright © Ziauddin Sardar 2016

Ziauddin Sardar has asserted his right under the Copyright, Designs and
Patents Act 1988 to be identified as the author of this work.

ISBN 978-1-84954-949-3

10 9 8 7 6 5 4 3 2 1

A CIP catalogue record for this book is available from the British Library.

Set in Stempel Garamond

Printed and bound in Great Britain by
CPI Group (UK) Ltd, Croydon CR0 4YY

Contents

Glossary

ADAB: literally, etiquette; more specifically the etiquette of being human. The literary and philosophical movement of classical Islam that established liberal humanism between the eighth and the thirteenth centuries.

DEOBANDI: an adherent of the revivalist movement that emerged from the Deoband seminary in India during the eighteenth century. The Deobandis are Sunni Muslims, puritan and close cousins of the Wahhabis.

HADITH: sayings or traditions of the Prophet Muhammad.

IJMA: literally, agreeing upon, consensus of the community in general, and (in recent history) the religious scholars in particular.

IJTIHAD: systematic original thinking; exerting oneself to the utmost degree to reach comprehension and form a rational opinion based on evidence.

ILM: knowledge in all forms, and distributive knowledge in particular, incorporating the notions of wisdom and justice. In contemporary times, it has been reduced to obscurantist religious knowledge.

ISLAMIC ORTHODOXY: an amalgam of Sunni and Shia Muslims who follow the strict theological and legal interpretations of classical theologians of eighth and ninth centuries and believe that these interpretations cannot be changed and that the Shariah is divine.

JIHAD: literally, striving. Any earnest striving in the way of God, involving personal, financial, intellectual or physical effort, for righteousness and against oppression or wrongdoing.

KHARJITES: a seventh-century fanatical and murderous sect.

MUTAZILA: the school of Islamic theology based on reason and rational thought that flourished from the eighth to the thirteenth centuries. The Mutazila laid the foundations of Islamic philosophy, established the movement of liberal humanism (*adab*) in Islam, and produced some of the greatest thinkers of civilisation (as we and others know it).

SAHIH AL-BUKHARI: the foremost authentic collection of hadith in Sunni Islam, compiled by the Persian scholar Muhammad al-Bukhari (810–870), during the ninth century.

SAHIH MUSLIM: the second most important collection of hadith in Sunni Islam, compiled by the Persian scholar Muslim ibn al-Hajjaj (815–875), during the ninth century.

SALAFI: member of an ultra-conservative, fanatical

movement in Sunni Islam based on the doctrine that the example of Prophet Muhammad and his earliest followers – the *salafs*, or 'pious forefathers' – should be followed and imitated totally and without question. Those who do not are heretic at best and infidels to boot at worse.

SHARIAH: literally the path to a watering hole; it is the ethical, moral and legal code of Islam. Conventionally translated as 'Islamic Law', the Shariah is considered divine by the orthodox and has remained unchanged since the ninth century.

SHIAISM: the second most important sect of Islam, which believes that the legitimate successor to the Prophet Muhammad was his cousin and son-in-law, Ali, and that all other successors must come from the Prophet's family.

SUFISM: the great mystical tradition of Islam that has produced boundless literature and spiritual insights. Sufi orders trace their chain of teachers right back to the Prophet Muhammad.

SUNNAH: literally, path or example, it applies particularly

to the example of the Prophet Muhammad and includes what he said, actually did and agreed to.

SUNNISM: the dominant, majority sect of Islam, which believes that the legitimate successor to the Prophet Muhammad was his closest companion and father-in-law, Abu Bakr.

TABLIGHIS: followers of the Tablighi Jammat, an evangelical movement that emerged in India in 1927. The Tablighis reduce Sunni Islam to six principles: faith, prayer, remembrance of God, treating Muslims with honour (as long as they are men), sincerity of intention, and going out to preach their creed. They shun politics and can be recognised by their chaotic facial furniture.

TAKFIRIS: Sunni Muslims who denounce other Muslims as apostates or unbelievers (*kafirs*). They don't like anybody except themselves. Takfiri jihadis are happy to kill all others, starting with other Muslims, and believe that suicide bombers are martyrs who receive a one-way ticket to paradise. Basically, they are psychotic. The so-called Islamic State of Iraq and Syria (ISIS) is a takfiri jihadi enclave.

ULAMA: religious scholars (for what they are worth, which is little).

UMMAH: the ensemble of Muslim individuals and communities forming an entity of common culture with common goals and aspirations, as well as certain self-consciousness, but not necessarily a coincident common polity.

WAHHABISM: a puritan, ultra-conservative sect in Sunni Islam, named after its founder Muhammad ibn Abd al-Wahhab (1703–92). It is now the state ideology of Saudi Arabia. The ideologies of violent extremists such as al-Qaida, the Taliban of Pakistan and Afghanistan, Boko Haram of Nigeria and al-Shabab of Somalia can all be traced back to Wahhabism and Saudi Arabia.

First words

TAKE TWO RECENT incidents. On 22 May 2013, Fusilier Lee Rigby was run down by a car and then brutally hacked to death by two recent converts to Islam, Michael Adebolajo and Michael Adebowale. Brandishing their knives, the murderers told the world that they had killed a British soldier as revenge for the killing of Muslims by the British Army. On 10 August 2011, Haroon Jahan, twenty-one, was killed along with two of his friends when they were deliberately run down by a car driven by Afro-Caribbean youths. Haroon died protecting his community during the month of Ramadan. In an atmosphere of rising tensions, with the police fearing revenge attacks and killings, Haroon's father, Tariq Jahan, diffused the situation with a few unscripted words of immense dignity: 'Why do we have to kill one another? Why are we doing this? I have lost my son. Step forward if you want to lose your sons. Otherwise, calm down and go home – please.'[1] As a Muslim, Jahan said, revenge was not part of his faith. But his faith gave him the strength and composure, as Bryan Appleyard noted in the *Sunday Times*, 'to make one of the great speeches of the twenty-first century'.[2]

We have two entirely different versions of Islam. One based on an old tradition of love and tolerance, perhaps drawing some inspiration from Sufism; the other on a more recent sectarian version that has no notion of humanity or ethics. The vast majority of Muslims are not all that different from Tariq Jahan. But there is little doubt that the jihadis are gaining ground, enticing young British Muslims to join the so-called Islamic State of Iraq and Syria

---

1   Michael Seamark, 'Grieving father's voice of sanity', Mail Online, 11 August 2011.

2   'Death of Haroon Jahan', *Sunday Times*, 14 August 2011.

(ISIS), and spreading murder and mayhem from Nigeria and Somalia to the Middle East, Pakistan and Indonesia, and across the West.

The reasons for the rise and rapid spread of jihadi Islam, as any academic will tell you, are varied and complex. But that does mean that we can't pin down a couple of key culprits. I am going to suggest that the root cause of fanaticism, violent extremism and paranoid jihadism is a single sect that has, like the killer gangs in *Mad Max* movies, gone berserk: Wahhabism. And we – the Muslims in general, and the British governments of past and present in particular – have nursed and nourished, supported and propped up the official site of this totalitarian creed for several decades: the police state and theocracy of Saudi Arabia.

Wahhabi dogma now occupies the central position in Islamic orthodoxy for a fundamental historical reason: the outright suppression of the great tradition of critical thinking and free thought in Islam. From the eighth to the fourteenth centuries, philosophers, writers, satirists and other freethinkers stood up to orthodoxy and curbed its authoritarian tendencies. But that tradition has now all but disappeared. And in its absence, Islamic orthodoxy has become more and more dogmatic, narrow, authoritarian and inhuman – reaching its logical culmination with the rise of Wahhabism. The guardians of Islamic orthodoxy, the *ulama*, the religious scholars and clerics, have banned criticism and question, stolen free will, and turned ordinary Muslim believers into empty vessels who have nothing more to do than gratefully receive and follow their hateful ideology.

Much of what I have to say about Islamic orthodoxy, traditionalism and Wahhabism will upset the bearded mullahs and legions of their pious and conservative followers. But as the eleventh-century Muslim thinker Al-Ghazali, perhaps the most reactionary theologian of the classical period and a key player in the decline of rational and free thought in Islam, once said, 'I am no longer obliged to remain silent.' Some may even accuse me of heresy. Which will put me in the good company of countless Muslim freethinkers, classical and contemporary, who had to endure such accusations. But in my case the accusation has more meaning – what I am actually suggesting is that it is time for heresy to take centre stage and to dethrone orthodoxy.

Those who follow my arguments would realise, I hope, that independent critical thinking and free thought is the only way to promote more rational and humane interpretations of Islam. It was the case when Muslim civilisation was at its zenith and individuals like Tariq Jahan were the dominant majority in every Muslim community. And it is the case even now, when orthodox dogma has created radical evil like ISIS and spouts characters like Michael Adebolajo, who threaten to end Muslim civilisation as we know it. Make no mistake: these dogmatic thugs hate rational and freethinking Muslims more than they hate non-Muslims or the West.

Part 1

Part I

What I am asked

BELLE VUE GIRLS' School in Bradford describes itself as 'a specialist academy for languages and science with maths', devoted to 'educating the women of tomorrow'. It is one of the highest-performing schools in the city, and, by Ofsted's ranking, always in the top 20 per cent of schools in the country when measured by the progress its pupils make from year seven to year eleven. Most of its 1,200 or so pupils are from Muslim backgrounds. I visited the school to have a 'candid conversation' with sixth formers pursuing religious studies. I had been roped into the schools programme of the Bradford Literature Festival, which ran for ten days in May 2015.

I arrived early on Friday morning expecting a relatively comfortable question-and-answer session. After a casual walk through the long school corridors I was ushered into a classroom. Over two dozen excited girls, some wearing hijabs, stood up to greet me. The teacher, Aqeela Jahan, a gracious, sublime English woman who had converted to Islam, asked them to sit down. I stood in front of the class as she uttered a few words of introduction. Today's topic, she said, was 'everything you wanted to ask about Islam but never dared'. Several hands shot up before she finished her sentence. I pointed towards a girl in hijab. 'How do we determine the will of God?' she asked in a matter-of-fact way. The question knocked me out of my comfort zone. I sat down on the small chair in front of the class to think of a viable answer.

The questions I am usually asked on such occasions tend to be straightforward. What are the five pillars of Islam? (Faith in a merciful and beneficent God; daily prayers; fasting during the month of Ramadan; zakat, or almsgiving; and hajj, the pilgrimage to Mecca if one has the means for the journey.) Does Islamic theology portray women as inferior to men? (No. Islam views men and women as equal before God 'created from a single soul' (The Qur'an 4:1, 39:6). But misogynist interpretations throughout history have relegated women to the kitchen.) Are Muslim men allowed to have four wives? (Only if they can be perfectly just to all of them, which is impossible. Most Muslim men have problems treating one fairly and ethically, so more than one is simply out of the question.) This sort of thing. But these pupils had already sorted most of these questions in their religious studies class.

When I had recovered my composure, I said: 'This is a difficult question. Perhaps we can start with a simple question.' Several girls raised their hands immediately, and I randomly pointed towards a pupil who oozed confidence. 'Would you say that Islam is incompatible with postmodernism?' she asked. There was no way I could duck the second question. 'Yes, it is,' I replied. 'Postmodernism suggests that almost everything that provides meaning and a sense of direction in our lives is meaningless – such as religion, history, tradition, reason and science. It also argues that all truth is relative. As a faith, Islam seeks to provide meaning and direction in the lives of believers. It places strong emphasis on tradition, history, reason and science.

And it sees only some truths as relative. Ironically, post-modernism itself functions as a religion for some people.' A lively discussion followed, with some girls expressing slight disagreement with my explanation. 'It wasn't nuanced enough,' said one.

Then we moved on to the difference between Sunni and Shia Islam. The real difference between them, I said, lies in political theology. After the death of the Prophet Muhammad a dispute emerged amongst his followers regarding the issue of succession. The Prophet himself did not designate his successor. So who had the legitimate claim to succeed him? One group argued that the successor should be chosen by election or selection from amongst his closest companions; this group called itself *Ahl as-Sunnah wa l-Jammah*, or the People of the Tradition of the Prophet and the Consensus of the Community (*ummah*), or Sunnis for short. But another group argued that only members of the family of the Prophet had the right to succeed him, and Ali, his cousin and son-in-law, was the only legitimate person to lead the Muslim community. This group was known as *Shiatu Ali*, the Party of Ali, and came to be known as Shia. Those who supported the Sunni view were in the majority and won the day.

The dispute was solidified in the political theology of each group. The Sunnis created a mythology around the companions, designating the first four caliphs as 'Rightly Guided', and insisting that the examples of all the companions had to be followed; and, after the companions, the companions of the companions. In contrast, the Shia created an edifice around the members of the Prophet's family, who were seen as immaculate and pure, unique and predetermined for each age, true believers who have to be recognised and followed if one is to be saved. These legitimate hirers to the Prophet's mantle were known as imams. Ali was the first imam, and his descendants, through the Prophet's youngest daughter Fatima, became subsequent imams. In total, there are twelve imams; and this is why the largest Shia community describes itself as 'Twelvers'. The last imam, Imam Mahdi, is said to have gone into occultation and will reappear towards the end of days to rid the world of evil. The Ismailis, a minority Shia sect, believe that there are only seven imams – hence, they are known as 'Seveners'.

Despite this contrived dogma, Shia and Sunnis are just different kinds of Muslim. All Shia are largely Sunnis, as they embrace all the basic tenets of Sunnism. All Sunnis are actually partly Shia, as demonstrating love for the Prophet and his family is as important in Sunni theology as it is in Shia. The only difference is that Sunnis demonstrate unconditional love for all the companions of the Prophet while the Shia limit their devotion to the circumference of the Prophet's family.

As one question followed another, it became evident that the sixth formers at Belle Vue Girls' School were into asking critical, complex questions. And they were not going to be satisfied with simple answers. Not the sort of women who will go and join the 'Islamic State of Iraq and the Levant' (ISIL) to become 'jihadi brides'. Not, then, like the three sisters who left for the so-called 'Islamic State' during half-term holiday on 28 May 2015. Khadija Dawood, Sugra Dawood and Zohra Dawood, who lived only a few miles from the school, took their nine children aged between three and fifteen with them. They told their husbands that they were going for the lesser pilgrimage, Umrah, to Mecca. But they headed straight for Syria instead.

What, I asked, did the Belle Vue sixth formers think of those who leave Britain to fight for the Islamic State? 'Misguided.' 'Brainwashed.' 'Not very educated, are they?'

The answers came quick and fast. Another girl in hijab said: 'They know very little about Islam. What they know they have acquired from the social media or websites run by ultra-conservative imams. They think they are learning about Islam but they are being fed propaganda and a literalist, extremist version of Islam.' Another lively discussion followed, and we ended up exploring the reasons why some young Muslims are happy to give up their lives in Britain and head for 'the Caliphate' in Syria.

The session with the sixth formers lasted four hours. I was exhausted; I had never been questioned, cross-examined and politely put down so thoroughly before. I felt like I had been forensically interrogated in a court of law. After the event, the teacher, Mrs Jahan, offered me a much needed cup of tea. What inspires these students, I wondered, to ask such searching questions? Clearly the school and the teacher had something to do with it. I learned from Mrs Jahan that there is considerable emphasis in her Islamic studies class on what is called 'philosophy for children'. It is not that she teaches Aristotle and Plato, or Hegel and Wittgenstein; rather, she teaches philosophical modes of learning and inquiry, of asking questions through discussion and debate. She encourages her pupils to read widely, to reflect on what they read, and to realise that they don't always have to be right. The girls who were firing questions at me from all directions obviously read widely. Indeed, they had even read a few of my books; one, a rather scholarly tome on postmodernism, was a set text and had been devoured thoroughly. And they knew how to ask questions – not just questions for the sake of questions, but questions that were based on thought and reflection. They were into critical engagement. That was the key difference between the sixth formers at Belle Vue Girls' School and those young men and women who trudged off to Syria in search of 'jihad'.

Over the past few years, I have gone out of my way to engage with young Muslims – from Bradford and Birmingham to Lahore and Istanbul. Everywhere, the young are restless and rebellious, eager to break out of convention, longing to be free from their parents and from tradition that crushes individual and social creativity and spirit. They are grappling with the challenges of modernity against tremendous odds, trying to discover what it means to be Muslim in the twenty-first century. They are angry at the plight of Muslims, at the wars in Iraq and Syria, at the invasion of Afghanistan, at the drone attacks in Pakistan, at the dehumanisation of the Palestinians by the Israelis, at the demonisation of Islam and Muslims. Frankly, I too would be angry at what has been done to Muslim societies in the name of 'modernity', 'democracy', 'our security' (as though the security and lives of others do not matter), 'war on terror', et cetera; and I do not count myself amongst the young.

Indeed, I *am* angry.

But just because they are angry and rebellious does not mean that they are about to take a nihilistic jump and join a death cult. Or support the aims and objectives of the 'Islamic State'. The majority of Muslims around the world, I believe, think, like the Belle Vue sixth formers, that the jihadis are deluded, misguided, brainwashed and just plain ignorant about Islam. Indeed, Muslims are as bewildered about the 'sudden' emergence of ISIS as everyone else. Just as they were at the atrocity that was 9/11. I remember my neighbour, the wonderful, straight-talking Bill, asking a few days after the aircraft attack on the Twin Towers: 'Zia, are these chaps from your lot?' 'Nothing to do with me, Bill,' I replied. 'But they are Muslims?' 'I suppose they are, since they describe themselves as Muslims. Just as the National Front types describe themselves as British.'

My Muslim friends often ask: why are all of us Muslims painted with the same brush? My answer has two parts. First, it is often forgotten that Muslims are a human community of 1.4 billion people. Just like any other human community, Muslims come with all shades of tendencies and opinions from one end of the spectrum to another – left wing, right wing, no wing, conservatives, liberals, secularists, not-so-secularists, democrats, autocrats, theocrats and extremists of various ilk. And Islam too is just as varied and broad. To suggest, argue, see, or represent Muslims or Islam in general as 'extremists', or 'anti-democracy', or prone to radicalisation, is to dehumanise around a quarter of the inhabitants of the planet. This inclination, which nowadays goes under the rubric of 'Islamophobia', gets a boost from a deeply rooted historical trend in the West known in scholarly circles as Orientalism[3] – the proclivity of representing Islam and Muslims as the darker side of Europe. Since way back in the Middle Ages, Orientalist scholars, writers, novelists, poets, artists and travellers have tried to show that Islam and Muslims are everything that the West is not: ignorant

---

3   See Ziauddin Sardar, *Orientalism*, Open University Press, Buckingham, 1999.

and stupid, cruel and barbaric, unclean and inferior, monstrous and ugly, fanatic and violent. This portrayal was not based on absence of knowledge but was a deliberately constructed ignorance. Of course, not all Orientalists engaged in this exercise; some contributed genuine knowledge both to Islamic thought and to the understanding of Islam in the West. But a trend was established that continues to this day. It is like the herpes virus. There is no cure for it as yet. Most of the time it lies dormant, stuck to the nether regions of the Western subconscious. But now and then something happens, say, a terrorist attack, and it is activated. The urge to scratch then becomes unbearable, and all the old Orientalist stereotypes about Islam and Muslims come to the fore. Right-wing, popular and quality press, racist websites and blogs, presidents, prime ministers and even some gentlemen in dog collars join in an orgy of Muslim bashing. Such representations not only deny the diversity of Muslims and varieties of Islam, they also impede our mutual understanding and become a barrier between human communities.

Muslims are an immensely diverse people. Even in Britain, the different ethnicities of Muslims are quite mind-boggling. Then there are numerous layers of sects, which are not always easy to differentiate – even for Muslims themselves. But the one variety of Muslims that concerns most people – the group that I am constantly asked about – is the 'fundamentalists'. These too come in a wide range of shades and tendencies. I often found it difficult to explain the complexity of fundamentalist thought and the sheer range of fundamentalist opinions and positions. Then, another group of school girls came to my rescue and made me realise that the religiosity of fundamentalist Islam, and the sectarian divisions that go with it, can actually be read and seen on the beards of Muslim men.

A typology of Muslim beards

I was on a bus, quietly reading, when a group of Muslim teenagers came and sat on the seats in front of me. There were six of them, all in black hijabs, and very rowdy. They were sixth formers from a London school that could not be more different than Bradford's Belle Vue Girls' School. They were simultaneously trying to balance their school bags and books in one hand, holding mobile phones in the other, texting or surfing the web, giggling and engaging in a strident conversation. 'Look at this,' one of them said, pointing to her phone. Other girls immediately peered at what I presumed to be a picture of some pop star. 'She looks like a *hijra* (transsexual), innit?' They laughed. Another girl pulled a picture from her mobile. 'It's me dad's new car; it's blue,' she said. 'But if someone says it's blue he gets upset.' She pulled her hijab, and said in a rather good mock accent: 'Why are you insulting my second wife? It's turquoise.' They all laughed. 'Me mum wants me to marry this American geezer,' one girl said. The others all tried to snatch the phone from her hand. 'American Muslims are like weird. They are all Tablighis. They go around converting people,' one of them said loudly, almost as if she was making a declaration to the whole bus. 'Is he a man or an elf?' one of them asked. 'Dream on, elf,' shouted another. 'Look at his beard! It goes all the way to his knees.' Everyone looked. 'He can say his *namaz* [a prayer] starkers!' Then one of them asked, almost as though she was thinking aloud, a perennial question: 'God, He has a beard, innit?'

A pertinent question, I thought. One that needed to be answered urgently. So as soon as I got back home, I sat down to pen an answer. Now, you may or may not know that I edit a quarterly intellectual magazine called

Critical Muslim. It deals with all things Islamic in an objective, questioning spirit. The aim is to seek new readings of Islam as well as its culture and civilisation and discover what it means to be a Muslim in the twenty-first century. My response to the question first appeared in the pages of *Critical Muslim*,[4] and I think segments of it are worth reproducing here. It also turned out to be a dangerous question. The issue of *Critical Muslim* with my essay on beards was banned in a number of Muslim countries. The most common explanation I received was that a disparaging discussion of Muslim beards is likely to inflame the conservatives, and could even usher in the wrath of the jihadis!

I suspect that God is fully furnished with a beard. He has created the world in His own image. That's why he has asked all those who worship Him to announce themselves with appropriate stubbles. All the great Prophets, Moses, Jesus and Muhammad, had beards. Those in charge of keeping the faith pure and unsullied, the rabbis, the priests and the mullahs, normally have beards. Hasidic Jews do not even trim their beards, let alone cut them. Ditto pious,

---

4   *Critical Muslim 3: Fear and Loathing*, Hurst, London, 2012 pp. 239–46.

God-fearing Sikhs. In Eastern Christianity, beards were recommended for the believers and were mandatory for the priesthood. Certain Christian sects, such as the Amish and Hutterite men, never sever their beards. For the mystics of all varieties – the Sufis, the Yogis and followers of Kabbalah – the beard is holy, the instrument that channels the grace of God (*barakah*) from above, where God presumably resides, to the human soul. For certain types of all-too-pious Muslims, a beard is obligatory, a legally constituted entity with its own rights and needs.

My own soul, I am sorry to report, has not been very accommodating to beards. Perhaps that's because I am not particularly pious. But I take comfort in the fact that the vast majority of Muslim men on this planet do not have beards. That does not mean that they are not devout; but it does suggest that they do not take their religion literally and tend to be – even if they happen to be rather conservative – a bit more open-minded. But beards matter to those who take their religion literally and very, very seriously. The point was brought home to me a few years ago when I visited the notorious Haqqani madrassa in the north Waziristan region of Pakistan. The madrassa is widely seen as a hotbed of jihadis, and the network of jihadis associated with or allied to the Taliban. The word *talib* means student; it is the students from this and other similar madrassas who constitute a variety of different groups collectively known as the Taliban. Inside the Haqqani madrassa, I was cornered by a bearded student. 'Are you a Muslim?' he asked me. 'It can be said that I am a Muslim,' I replied. 'So why don't you have a beard?' I replied that I did not think it was necessary for Muslim men to have a beard. 'But it is a religious requirement,' he shot back. I pointed out that it was not in the Qur'an. The Sacred Text has quite a few categorical statements and direct injunctions. For example, 'there is no compulsion in religion' (2:256); although the bearded ones have interpreted it to mean there is compulsion in religion – the very fact that you have to have a beard is compulsion enough, in my opinion. Or 'free the slave' (90:13; 2:177), which the bearded ones never did, much to the shame of Muslim civilisation. So the Qur'an could easily have stated, I pointed out to the student, 'Grow a beard.' Which it doesn't. But that was not enough for the student. He would not let me go.

'Do you follow the example of the Prophet?' he asked forcefully. 'Yes,' I replied, 'when it is possible.' 'The

Prophet had a beard, and if you follow his examples you would have a beard.' By now he was almost shouting at me. 'But if blades were available he would have used them,' I shouted back in reply.

The Prophet Muhammad did indeed have a beard, and the sanction for the beard comes from the traditions of the Prophet. There are sections on the subject in hadith, authentic collections of his sayings, such as the canonical text *Sahih Muslim*. They contain hadith like: 'The Messenger of Allah (peace be upon him) said: "Act against the polytheists, trim closely the moustache and grow the beard."' Now according to *The Masail of the Hair*, which for the uninitiated is 'A Short Treatise Explaining the Laws of Hair, Nails and Dyeing of the Hair',[5] a copy of which I was fortunate enough to acquire at my local Islamic bookshop, this is a universal command. 'The shaving or trimming of the beard is a major sin' and the beardless are doomed to hell.

However, it is probably worth mentioning that seventh-century Arabia was not a particularly diverse place. Everyone – Jews, Christians, Muslims, the polytheists

---

5 Idara Ishaat-e-Diniyat, Delhi, 1994.

and the 'fire worshippers' mentioned in *Sahih Muslim* – dressed and looked the same. This was a bit of a problem when you had to distinguish the Muslims from non-Muslims. For example, when the Muslims were caught in a pincer movement during the 625 Battle of Uhad, and the enemy approached both from front and behind, the Muslims were unable to distinguish who was who, and started to fight each other. So it made sense for them to physically stand out from their enemies. The facial furniture served the function of a military uniform. It made perfect sense in the specific context. I suspect that the Prophet would have provided his followers with military uniforms, if they had been available. He loved perfume, which was available in Mecca and Medina, and asked the believers to use it. He would have advised his followers to use twin blade razors (but not the three- or five-blade ones, which are totally useless), if they too were widely available.

The literalist would have us believe that everything the Prophet did or liked or disliked has universal import. He rode a camel, but even the literalists prefer to use a more modern means of transport. He fought with swords, but they are not much use in the age of guns and bombs. If we follow this logic we end up in a surreal universe, as demonstrated so well by a Pakistani mullah, supporting a huge beard. The Prophet, the mullah announced on Dunya TV, a popular satellite channel in Pakistan, liked the pumpkin. As such, all Muslims are duty bound to like the pumpkin. Those who don't, he declared, are not following *sunnah*, the example of the Prophet, not demonstrating their love for him, and therefore should be put to the sword.[6] The pumpkin, the Prophet's favourite vegetable, is more valuable and sacred than human life!

The beard has thus acquired cosmic importance in certain, well-defined, Muslim circles. It serves a number of important purposes. It's a badge of identity: it announces that the individual takes his religion extremely seriously, he follows what he thinks is the example of the Prophet to the letter, and he wishes to stand out from the rest of Muslim society. The shape, size and length of the beard proclaims the sect of the person who is supporting it. It makes a particular statement of ritual piety or political stance, which is used to shape group identity and create cohesion. This process is known as 'cultural cognition': what it means is that people form opinions about what

---

6 http://www.youtube.com/watch?v=vcDIlIRupqY.

is right or wrong not from facts and evidence but in line with their existing prejudices and cultural types – of which beards are an integral part. In literalist Muslim context, the beard announces: 'You can trust what I say. I share the same values as you. You do not need to listen to others outside our own group. I will reinforce your self-image.' That's why beards only listen to other beards, reinforcing group personality and prejudice.

For the fundamentalists, the beards provide a simple and straightforward answer to the cardinal question raised by the sixth formers of Belle Vue Girls' School: 'How do we determine the will of God?' The answer: it is to be found in a literalist reading of the Qur'an and explicit adherence to (what they imagine are) the examples, sayings and actions of the Prophet. And they suggest – indeed, some insist – that other Muslims need not bother raising this question because they have already determined the will of God. Moreover, as the pious, bearded ones, who follow the example of the Prophet to the letter, God has given them special authorisation to convey His will to all and sundry.

What distinguishes one particular type of beard from another depends on how this self-proclaimed authority is exercised. In Britain, you will encounter four basic types of Muslim beards, each quite distinct and broadcasting its own particular message.

1. THE TABLIGH

This is a full, long, untrimmed, unruly beard of chaotic proportions, without a moustache (which is considered a sign of arrogance). It is obligatory amongst the members of the Tablighi Jamaat, an evangelical movement that has mosques throughout Britain. It is, following the rules of chaos theory, a fractal beard. That is to say it looks the same from all directions: absurd. The most famous Tablighi beard in the world belongs to the captain of South Africa's cricket team, Hashim Amla. Amongst cricketing fans, Amla's beard is endowed with supernatural powers, and attracts as much attention as his batting, which is truly remarkable. Unfortunately, the same cannot be said of his beard, replicas of which can be bought easily at any match involving South Africa. 'The optimum length for me, as a Muslim,' Amla told a *Guardian* journalist, 'is for the beard to be of fist-length.'[7] Which makes you wonder: just how long is Amla's fist? 'I love it when guys ask me

---

7   *The Guardian*, 8 July 2008.

about Islam or my beard. To share knowledge is a duty,' he says. So for Amla, his beard is an invitation to Islam, to all that is good and wholesome. In Britain, we have our own favourite Tablighi beard, which sits proudly on the face of Moeen Ali, the English international cricketer. Like Amla and Ali, most Tablighi beards take their religion, and their cricket, seriously but hate politics. They tend to be rather conservative and obsessed with rituals and they abhor strife and violence. They believe that a righteous life should be devoted to prayer, fasting and inviting people to Islam. They have a tendency to build huge (but, it has to be said, rather ugly) mosques such as the one proposed in the London borough of Newham, which was supposed to have four times the capacity of St Paul's Cathedral. Mercifully, the project has been rejected.

For the Tablighis, Islam consists of just six points: correct belief, regular prayer, praising God, sincerity of intention, respect for other Muslims and devoting time to preaching. All human problems, Tablighi Jamaat tells its followers, can be solved by prayer and proselytising.

However, in the Tablighi framework, respect for other Muslims does not include respect for women. The Tablighis are aggressively misogynist, a point well illustrated by Junaid Jamshed, a former Pakistani rock star who now runs a Muslim charity that is based less than a mile from my humble abode in north-west London. Jamshed made his name as the lead singer of the highly successful rock band Vital Signs. On my visits to Pakistan during the late 1980s and 1990s, I discovered that it was practically impossible to ignore Vital Signs – their songs were constantly being played on television and radio, on buses and in the bazaars. In particular, their unofficial Pakistani anthem, 'Dil Dil Pakistan' ('My Heart is Pakistan'), was exceptionally popular. After the band broke up, Jamshed transformed himself into a designer, established his own clothing brand, and opened a string of stores in Karachi, Lahore and Islamabad, selling traditional garments for men and women designed with a subtle hint of modernity. I bought a couple of rather suave kameez shalwar suits from one of his outlets in Lahore (they are called 'J.' – J dot) that I wear at weddings or on other occasions when I want to show off my sophisticated Pakistani heritage.

After the turn of the millennium, Jamshed was suddenly hit by a divine thunderbolt, had 'a turn of heart with Allah's blessing', and joined the Tablighi Jamaat. He grew an outrageous beard and began preaching. In general, his sermons, widely available on YouTube, emphasise prayer, fasting and treating others with dignity and respect. But, being a Tablighi, he takes every opportunity to reprimand women for not dressing properly, or for displaying their hair, or for speaking in public, or for not being in the kitchen tending to the family's needs. In November 2014, while explaining why women are inferior to men, he related a story about Ayesha, the youngest wife of the Prophet Muhammad. In the story, which may or may not be authentic, Ayesha pretends to be ill to attract the attention of her husband. Jamshed concludes the story by declaring that 'a woman cannot be reformed even if she is in the gathering of the Prophet'. Not surprisingly, his comments caused an uproar. The conservative beards saw his remark as disrespectful to Ayesha, even blasphemous. The inevitable threats followed. Jamshed apologised but I suspect he will not be visiting Pakistan any time soon.[8]

2. THE TASHBIH

Long and flowing, usually white, sometimes attached to a turban on the head. The Tashbih should not be confused

---

8   The whole story can be read, and viewed, at http://showbizpak.com/junaid-jamshed-blasphemy-comment-for-hazrat-aisha-than-apology-video.

with *tasbih*, which is a prayer bead; although I imagine hair in one's beard could also be used for enumerating the Ninety-Nine Beautiful Names of God. The Tashbih, a Father Christmas-like rug, is said to be 'a beard made of love'. The word itself means anthropomorphism, and the beard is meant to display human characteristics of God. It is a common sight in mystical circles, where life revolves around the pursuit of mystical union with God. On the whole, those supporting this beard are not interested in worldly affairs; they tend to spend most of their time in *zikr*, or remembrance of Allah, poring over classical texts and debating the finer points of Islamic calligraphy. However, there have been cases in Britain where the Tashbih-sporting Sufis, or Pirs as they are known amongst the British of Pakistani heritage, have turned out to be charlatans. The Tashbih can be seen gracing the faces of many contemporary British Sufis such as Shaykh Hisham Kabbani, who is the head of the Naqshbandi tariqa, or branch, of Sufism. (The other equally famous Sufi, Shaykh Abdal Hakim Murad (aka T. J. Winter), dean of Cambridge's Muslim College, supports a gentle wispy affair, a shy net curtain rather than a floating rug.)

In Britain, the Sufi tradition is dominated by the

Barelvis, a South Asian movement devoted to the (often irrational) love of the Prophet. The Barelvis believe that the Prophet was a special kind of man: he was human but created from light; while dead, he is still very much alive and present everywhere, and he has knowledge of the future. Most of their ritual practices revolve around these beliefs – they celebrate the birthday of the Prophet with great pomp and ceremony, visit the Prophet's mosque in Medina, Saudi Arabia, visit the tombs of his companions and saints, and think that shaving the beard is a cardinal sin.

But we will do great injustice to Sufism if we simply equate it with the Barelvi tradition. Sufism has a long, rich and distinguished history in Islam and has produced some of the greatest thinkers and poets of Muslim thought and literature, such as the prolific and original thinker, the thirteenth-century Sufi Ibn Arabi, who critiqued patriarchy and sexism and developed an ethics of what it means to be human. Ibn Arabi argued that masculinity and femininity are mere accidents of birth and do not belong to the essence of human nature, which is one. Women can be imams and lead prayers in the mosque, create religious and legal precedent and become leaders of the community. And a man is not a man unless he becomes a woman in his soul.

Or the brilliant mystic and master story-teller, Rumi, the thirteenth-century founder of the Mevlevi Order of the Dancing Dervishes. For Rumi, Islam was nothing more or less than pure love, as expressed in his lyrical poetry, epigrams and short stories, some of which are collected in the vast compendium of his teaching, *The Masnavi*. In one charming story, he captures the essence of how 'the will of God' has been manipulated and appropriated by all types of beards.

A thief climbed a tree in an orchard and started to eat its fruit. He was spotted by the owner. 'Hey, you scoundrel!' shouted the owner. 'Aren't you ashamed before God? Why are you stealing my fruit?' 'If', the thief retorted, 'the servant of God eats from the orchard of God, the dates God has given him, why do you blame him? Why do you behave so miserly at the table of so rich a Master?'

The owner asked his servant to bring a rope and a stick. 'I'll give a proper answer to you, my friend.' He tied the thief with the rope, and set about him with the stick, beating him on the back and legs. 'Have some shame before God!' cried the thief. 'You are beating an innocent person.' 'With the stick of God,' the owner replied, 'this servant of

God is thrashing the back of another servant of God. The stick is God's, the back and sides are God's. I am the servant and instrument of His command.'[9]

While the Tablighis tend to subtract from the sum of human knowledge, the Sufis have an enviable record of promoting tolerance and pluralism as well as poetry, literature and art. The Tabligh and the Tashbih can thus be seen as benign; both suggest that the will of God is understood as love of God and our fellow men (albeit, the women are often excluded) and the instrument for our concern is politeness, geniality and compassion. But pitted against them are two types of beards that are quite dangerous.

3. THE MAHMAL

A combination of the goatee and the moustache, but the two are not connected. Sometimes the goatee is as wide as the mouth, giving the illusion that it is the beard that

---

9   There are numerous translations of Rumi's *Masnavi*. The best, rather old, are *Discourses of Rumi* (John Murray, London, 1961) by A. J. Arberry, and *Teachings of Rumi*, abridged and translated by E. H. Whinfield (Octagon Press, London, nd). I have used Peter Washington's *Rumi*, an Everyman edition (Alfred Knopf, New York, 2006), which selects the best from a combination of translations. 'The Thief in the Orchard' is on page 101.

does all the talking. The Mahmal is best seen on the faces of Saudi monarchs: see the photographs of the late Kings Abdulaziz, King Fahd or King Abdullah. The sculpted, sophisticated nature of the Mahmal symbolises wealth and power. I have labelled it after the palanquin that the Mamluk sultans and Ottoman caliphs sent to Mecca with each pilgrim caravan to assert their sovereignty over the holy places. Like the palanquin, which was designed for one person, the Mahmal reflects a single, correct and indisputable, view of Islam that, the beard tells us, by the grace of God, will become sovereign over the globe. And, like its namesake, it comes with largesse that is generously distributed to those who follow the Wahhabi path and equip themselves with appropriate mental and physical apparatus. I am reliably informed that there are beard farms in Saudi Arabia, at the Universities of Mecca and Medina, where it is grown in abundance and is worn by a plethora of clerics who issue regular fatwas, such as the samosa is *haram* (forbidden) because it resembles a cross, or women are not permitted in Shariah, or Islamic law, to shave their moustache (I am not making this up). If the Wahhabis have their way, we will all, men and women, be wearing the Mahmal.

4. THE CURTAIN

A close associate of the Mahmal, this is a thick, busy affair that shrouds the face. Shorter than the Tabligh, it is usually groomed and trimmed, but not as sophisticated as the Mamhal. It is de rigueur in politicised Muslim circles. You will find it gracing the faces of people generally referred to as 'Islamists' – that is, belonging to global Islamic revivalist movements characterised by literalism and moral conservatism that see Islam as 'a total system'. It is standard facial furniture for the Deobandis, a revivalist movement from India, the followers of Jamaat-e-Islami, an Islamist revivalist movement from Pakistan, and the more pious members of the Muslim Brotherhood, the Islamist movement of Egypt. It is also worn by more extremist groups such as Hizb ut-Tahrir, the global movement of Islamists that seeks to establish a caliphate. Like the hijab (and other variants such as purdah, niqab and chador), which hides a woman's beauty, the Curtain, too, hides something in men that should not be displayed in public: authoritarian ugliness. This is really a potent beard, as it can drive the person supporting the Curtain into a maddening pursuit of the 'Islamic state' ruled by the Shariah, much like Saudi Arabia.

In Britain, the most noted Curtain belongs to Anjem Choudary, who established and led the minuscule extremist group al-Muhajiroun. It can also be found adorning more respectable, and allegedly 'moderate', faces such as the folks who manage and run the Islamic Foundation in Leicester, the stronghold of Jamaat-e-Islami in Britain (they may deny it but their beards speak volumes). In the 'Islamic movement' circles, the Curtain is seen as a sign of masculinity, higher status, religious authority and even wisdom.

(For the sake of completeness, we should also mention the Beard That Is Not Really a Beard. In most cases, it is a functional beard like the one that graces the face of Jeremy Corbyn. But in some cases it acquires a higher significance, much like Duchamp's urinal that became a 'Fountain' when it was placed in an art gallery. It becomes a beard that is grown in protest at all other beards. Mostly worn by young, hip, professional British Muslim men, who have learned to use electric shavers with considerable skill (it is not easy to get that elusiveness quite right), it is nothing more than designer stubble. It is designed to make a statement or express a particular mood: I do not support the fundamentalists, I am open-minded and multicultural,

I am feeling like an intellectual, I am protesting against the bearded ones as well as those who demonise Muslims, I am a fashion-conscious, liberal, young Muslim.)

Extreme beards

Now, the Mahmal and the Curtain are two distinct beards, but they are based on the same ideology: Wahhabism. It started as a theological reform movement with the goal of bringing Muslims back to 'pure Islam'. The movement was started in Saudi Arabia by the eighteenth-century theologian Muhammad ibn Abd al-Wahhab, who regarded Sufi practices, such as venerating saints and visiting shrines, as an innovation in Islam – 'innovation' here meaning a deviation from purity and therefore to be avoided. To preserve the purity of Islam, Abd al-Wahhab argued, the Muslims must adhere to a very strict and literal interpretation of the Qur'an and the examples of the Prophet. The will of God was clear and precise. Everything else, including the interpretations set out by all other sects, comprised innovations (*bida*), or apostasy (*ridda*), or downright denial of God (*kufr*). Thus, art, music, dance, theatre and other cultural expressions were an innovation. Mixing of sexes, particularly in public places, was a cardinal crime. Philosophy and critical questioning, or following the schools of Islamic thought, verged on apostasy. Images and portrayal of the human body were akin to idolatry and were thus a declaration of unbelief.

Abd al-Wahhab's followers, who regard themselves as the cornerstone of Sunni orthodoxy, came to be known as Wahhabis. However, to differentiate themselves from other claimants of orthodox Sunnism, the Wahhabis call themselves Salafis – that is, they model themselves on the earliest followers and companions of the Prophet, known as *al-salaf al-salih*, the pious forefathers. If, for some reason, the companions of the Prophet cannot be followed, the Wahhabis argued, then Muslims must follow the companions of the companions (*tabi'in*), and the next generation of follower's followers (*tabi'i al-tabi'in*). Imitation is all that the Muslims can do; there can be no new thought or interpretations. The entire history and culture of Muslim civilisation is rejected as deviancy and degeneration. The Wahhabis regard anyone not adhering to Wahhabi beliefs and practices, including all other Muslims but particularly the Shia, as hostile dwellers in the domain of unbelief. In denying the right of a Muslim to question, to think, to explore,

Wahhabism has reduced religion to a simple comply/ not comply formula and a must-do list derived from the thought of dead bearded men, now guarded and enforced by living bearded men. The love of God emphasised by Sufism and other interpretations is now replaced by fear of God. But it is not just God but everyone and everything that has to be feared. Women have to be feared – lest they mislead men – and are thus totally marginalised in society as a whole, denied basic rights and compelled to cover themselves, from head to toes, in black shrouds. Muslims of other denominations have to be feared, for they may promote 'innovations', apostasy, and lead the Muslim community towards unbelief. People of other faiths, and no faith, have to be feared, as they may damage the true believers. Culture has to be feared, as it could undermine the one true faith. All variety of thought and dissent has to be feared and has to be punished severely. Indeed, if you had a beard that was unlike theirs, you would automatically be declared an apostate or a kafir and become a legitimate target of their violence. The Wahhabis believe that a human face can support only a single type of beard. Other varieties are deviations, innovations, perversions that cannot be allowed to mushroom.

It is important to realise that the Wahhabis are not a new phenomenon in Islamic history. The Wahhabi ideology of the eighteenth century is actually based on a rebel sect that emerged during the formative phase of Islam in the seventh century. This sect was known as the Kharjites, or 'the outsiders'. It believed that history had come to an end after the revelation to the Last Prophet Muhammad. The will of God had been disclosed once and for all times. From now on, no debate or compromise was possible on any question. To be a Muslim, the Kharjites argued, is to be in a perfect state of soul. Someone in that state cannot commit a sin or engage in wrongdoing. Any Muslim who sins, which includes political offences, is an apostate. Since the Kharjites considered themselves to be ideal Muslims, those who disagreed with them, or their politics, were automatically branded apostates – who could be put to death. This philosophy can be summed up as follows: live by the will of God which we have defined, give all to God, die for God, kill for God all those who disagree with you or stand in your way and you will have meaning and purpose in your life and paradise in your death. The Wahhabis are basically neo-Kharjites.

Wahhabism has three main characteristics. First, like the Kharjites, the Wahhabis believe that history ends with the Prophet Muhammad. As such, the worldview of Wahhabism is ahistorical. Wahhabis abhor history, and see Islam as a utopia that exists outside history. Nothing that has happened since the time of the Prophet and his pious companions, including the great thought, learning and culture of Islam and its civilisation, is of any significance. Wahhabism has no concept of human progress, moral development or evolution.

Second, Wahhabism has no notion of ethics; it drains Islam of all ethical contents. Thus, anything can be justified in the name of God, as an expression of the will of God. Intolerance, misogyny, floggings, beheading and xenophobia, as well as violations of basic human rights and violence, can be justified as divine will. Third, the state is unaccountable to anyone but God, whose will it exercises through the Shariah, or 'Islamic law'. The Shariah provides the state with the only legitimacy it needs, and as long as the state enforces the Shariah no one can legitimately overthrow it. Party politics, democracy and other such 'secular' concerns have no place in the state.

Back to our typology of beards. While most of those

who support the Mahmal and the Curtain subscribe to Wahhabi ideology, they do not necessarily follow the same approach to implementing the will of God. Consider, for example, Jamaat-e-Islami, which was established in British India in 1941. Since the 1947 partition, the Jamaat has systematically campaigned to turn Pakistan into an 'Islamic state'. Abul A'la Maududi (1903–79), the founder and the leader of the Jamaat till his death in 1949, saw Islam as a total system that regulates every aspect of human behaviour – from personal to social, economic to political, intellectual to psychological, from birth to death. Maududi argued that Islam and the state are inherently linked. Islam is not just the religion of the state but is also the state itself governed by the Shariah – 'the law of God'. And the best people to rule the state are experts on the Shariah, the *ulama* or the religious scholars, who are simultaneously the guardians of religion and the managers of the state.

But the best way to unite Islam and state into a single entity was democracy. Thus, while Jamaat-e-Islami is a Wahhabi movement, it is also a democratic one. Indeed, it has been contesting elections in Pakistan for decades with, thankfully, very little success. In contrast, its fellow Wahhabi travellers, the Muslim Brotherhood, were considerably more successful in Egypt. In the 2011 Egyptian parliamentary elections, the political wing of the Brotherhood, the Freedom and Justice Party, won a majority. The presidential election was won by the Brotherhood leader, Mohamed Morsi. However, once in power, the Brotherhood revealed its true Wahhabi colours: it tried to impose on Egypt, under the slogan 'Allah is our objective' (that is: we are implementing the will of God), an authoritarian, exclusivist, Shariah-based version of Islam. Egypt's generals weren't quite finished: Morsi was overthrown and the army returned to power. The counterparts of Jamaat-e-Islami and Muslim Brotherhood in Bangladesh, Malaysia, Indonesia, Tunisia, Morocco and other countries also ostensibly subscribe to democracy, and in Malaysia, Morocco and Tunisia they have had some success in becoming or getting close to the government.

Other Wahhabi sects mix democracy with militancy. A good example is Hizb ut-Tahrir, which has a strong presence in Britain. Established in 1953, it aims to bring all Muslims under a single Islamic state, or caliphate. The Palestinian founder of the global movement, Taqiuddin al-Nabhani (1909–77), had a few Sufi inclinations, so his brand of Islam advocates a fusion of traditional Sufi teachings – minus the love of others – with the political ideology of Wahhabism. It is the will of God, he declared, that all Muslims must live in a single unitary state, headed by an elected caliph. When the time is right, and Muslims are well prepared, the movement will assume power – by force if necessary. In contrast to the Jamaat-e-Islami or Muslim Brotherhood, Hizb ut-Tahrir is not interested in appealing directly to the masses. It targets key individuals – politicians, judges, lawyers, military officers, professors, industrialists and teachers – who are deemed important for its cause. They in turn are then expected to spread the word through their professional and social networks. The ideal path is to gain power with the assistance of important members of a targeted country.

Both the Mahmal and the Curtain have an in-built biological on/off switch. When the switch is off, the Beards behave as normal, and can even appear pleasant and amiable. But when the switch flips, it generates an uncontainable urge to display and flaunt the Beard's devotion to His will for all to fear. The most notable of these beards where the switch is definitely on belong to the Salafis. Most Salafis hate everything about the world – they hate all other Muslims for not being Good Muslims (that is, like them); they hate all Muslim countries for not being 'Islamic states', and, most of all, they hate the West for being everything they are not. In general, this hatred is largely confined to aggressive abuse and berating of all others. But there are some Salafis who are not satisfied with verbal gestures, who advocate active, offensive jihad against all those whom they perceive as their enemies; they regard it as a fundamental principle of Islam.

So we come to the most dangerous beards of all: Salafi jihadists. These too come in two flavours: Salafis who want to wage jihad against the West, perceived as an imperialist power out to destroy them; and those who accuse other Muslims of *takfir*, meaning they are apostates and thus legitimate targets of jihad. These are dubbed Salafi-takfiris. These repulsive beards have perverted the concept of just war in Islam.

It is worth tackling another common question I am asked: what is jihad?

Varieties of jihad

Jihad is perhaps the most used and abused term in contemporary Islamic parlance. The word itself, and its variants, appear throughout the Qur'an, where it is used to mean 'to struggle' or 'to exert oneself'. Nowadays, it is assumed, by Muslims and non-Muslims alike, that jihad is synonymous with fighting or war. But the terms for 'war' used in the Qur'an are totally different. When the Qur'an means war it uses two specific words, *al-harb* or *al-qital*. Somehow, both classical and modern commentators on the Qur'an forgot to mention this, and jihad and warfare have become one and the same. Worse: jihad is frequently glossed as 'holy war', as if there can be anything holy about violence.

Classical Muslim scholars were fond of categorising and classifying things. So they divided jihad into two broad categories: the greater struggle and the lower struggle. This division is based on something that the Prophet Muhammad once did. When he saw some soldiers returning from the battlefield he is reported to have said: 'Blessed are those who have performed the lesser struggle and have yet to perform the greater one.' He was asked: 'What is the greater struggle?' He replied: 'The struggle of the self.' This hadith has led to a general consensus amongst the classical scholars that the greatest jihad is against one's own ego, greed, lust and other human imperfections.

The lesser jihad, *al-jihad al-asghar*, also comes in two

varieties: defensive and offensive. The Muslim community is permitted to defend itself if attacked. The Qur'an declares: 'Fight in the way of Allah against those who fight you and do not transgress, certainly God loves not the aggressors' (2:190). The emphasis is on not transgressing, by which is meant not committing atrocities, not killing women, children and non-combatants, not burning down property or destroying people's livelihood, and responding disproportionately. For this is the way to self-destruction: 'Do not with your own hands hurl yourself to destruction' (2:195). Moreover, if the enemy ceases fighting, the Muslims have to lay down their weapons; only hostility is to be met with hostility. Thus defensive jihad is based on the principle of necessity and is for resistance, not to exterminate the enemy but only to persuade them to cease hostilities.

Offensive jihad is basically struggle against all forms of injustice. It has four levels: struggle with the heart, struggle with the tongue, struggle with wealth and struggle with one's soul. If you cannot do anything about the acts of oppression and injustices you witness in the world, you should at least despise them in your heart. And if you can, you should speak against them with your tongue: speak truth to power. If this is not possible, then you should support and promote resistance to injustice with your wealth. Finally, if you are able then you should fight with your soul – physically engage with the unjust.

In classical Muslim jurisprudence, the last option comes with a string of conditions. Physical jihad is still jihad in the name of God, so it cannot be an act of aggression, which is forbidden by the Qur'an. It cannot be a jihad for the benefit, utility or material gains of a state. One group of Muslims cannot declare jihad on another group of Muslims. The decision to undertake jihad cannot be based on the whims of an individual or some authoritarian or demented ruler but has to have the *ijma* or the consensus of the whole community – a consensus that is reached after much debate and discussion. There has to be a reasonable probability of success; it is not a suicide mission. And during conflict, the essential conditions of defensive jihad must also apply to offensive jihad: the values of life, property and human rights must be preserved.

The highly sophisticated and nuanced notion of jihad has been thoroughly debased by the Salafi jihadists. The notion of jihad as perpetual war against all, Muslims and non-Muslims alike, along with its new instruments such as suicide bombing, is a recent perversion. It emerged after the Soviet–Afghan war that began in December 1979 and lasted more than nine years, till February 1989. Muslims throughout the world saw this as a defensive jihad against an enemy hell-bent on suppressing and oppressing them. All sorts of Muslims from all varieties of Islamic groups joined the Afghan freedom fighters – mujahedeen – to fight on behalf of Afghanistan. Islamists from Algeria and Egypt, Wahhabis and Salafis from Saudi Arabia and the Gulf states, and puritan, simple-minded students from Pakistani madrassas came to support the struggle. The students came to be known collectively as Taliban, a term which literarily means pupils of madrassas. During the Afghan jihad, they were more or less united, but have since splintered into many groups. All of these jihadis from different countries and ethnic backgrounds were actively supported by the United States, Pakistan and Saudi Arabia: the first supplied the weapons, the second provided the local fighters, and the third looked after their finances. The different religious ideologies of various participants blended to produce a new variation: the traditionalism of the Afghans, the Salafism and Wahhabism of the Saudis, the radicalist Islamism of

the Algerians and the puritanism of Pakistani Taliban
produced the deadly combination of takfiri jihadism.
Wahhabism deprived these groups of all ethical concerns.
Salafism inducted them into hatred of all others. Islamism provided them with all the justification they needed
to do whatever it took, however abhorrent, to pursue the
goal of establishing an 'Islamic state' under the Shariah.
Puritanism gave them a sense of moral superiority: they
were enacting the will of God and therefore God would
reward them for their actions. All the teachings of the
Qur'an, the enlightened examples of the Prophet, as well
as the thought and learning of classical scholars, were
swept aside.

After the Afghan war was over, this new and deadly
notion of jihad was exported to other regions. New fronts
were created in the West as well as within the Muslim
world itself against religious and secular regimes. The
Saudis established al-Qaida, led by the Wahhabi Osama
bin Laden, and declared jihad on the West. The Taliban
declared Pakistan an infidel state and turned against
it. The Algerians returned to Algeria to engage in civil
war of unspeakable brutality and violence that began in
1991 after a military coup that undermined the election

victory of Islamic Salvation Front (FIS). Others found their way to Iraq, where a brutal assault was made on the Shia community.

Since then, the takfiri jihadi virus has spread far and wide with astonishing speed. It has become more and more virulent at each stage. In Pakistan itself the Taliban have splintered into a plethora of intrinsically violent subgroups such as Jamaat-ul-Ahrar, Lashkar-e-Taiba and Sipah-e-Sahaba who massacre school children, bomb mosques and churches, and target minority sects such as Shia and Ahmadi with their murderous campaigns. In Nigeria, the Boko Haram (meaning 'Western education is forbidden') engage in mass abductions, kidnap young girls to sell them into slavery, and indiscriminately kill civilians. In Somalia, the al-Shabab (meaning 'youth') hijack ships, slay tourists, attack shopping malls and terrorise villages. All of these groups present themselves as the instruments of the will of God.

So now we arrive at what the German philosopher Immanuel Kant would describe as 'radical evil': the jihadis of ISIS. But what do we call those depraved enough to see evil as good, who have internalised evil in their heart, and who see the dissemination of evil as their duty?

ISIS and Mad Max jihadis

'What is ISIS?' I was asked this at a meeting of university students in Lahore. I realised that they had not heard the term ISIS which we have used in Britain; they referred to ISIS as Daesh. The US and UN use the acronym ISIL ('Islamic State in Iraq and the Levant'). Others describe it simply as 'Islamic State'. Our own Prime Minister was not sure what to call this entity, and our national broadcaster, the BBC, was equally baffled. So by some sort of heavenly decree we have settled for 'the so-called Islamic State' – although I still favour ISIS.

The confusion arises from the Arabic term *al-Sham*, which can be translated as Syria, the Levant, or even Damascus. The jihadis who now occupy segments of Iraq and Syria describe their state in Arabic as *al-Dawla al-Islamiya fi Iraq wa al-Sham*, from which the acronym Daesh is derived. *Al-Dawla* is Arabic for state, normally used for a secular state. In Pakistan, and elsewhere in the Muslim world, the term is used derogatively, with a little bit of irony as in Urdu and Hindi Daesh translates as 'nation'.

Where does this 'so-called Islamic state' come from, I am asked. The question is raised not just by perplexed non-Muslims but also, and more frequently, by horrified Muslims. I have talked about ISIS with Muslims from Morocco to Indonesia, and everywhere the very mention of the term elicits expression of unrestrained repulsion and perplexity. Most people seem to think it has appeared from 'nowhere'. The impression is reinforced by the rapidity with which the jihadis conquered the land they now occupy – within two years they appear to have a functioning state. The bafflement stems from the fact that most people find the whole phenomenon of ISIS unbelievable, as though it was a piece of fiction. And it does appear as though the leader of ISIS and his followers have stepped out of the film *Mad Max: Fury Road*. The so-called caliph, or *Amir al-Muminin* ('Leader of the Faithful') Abu Bakr al-Baghdadi, sees himself as a Messiah figure, much like Immortan Joe, the villain-in-chief of *Mad Max*. Both have a proclivity for sexual perversion. Immortan keeps five 'wives' locked in a tower. He has shaped a state for himself and now wants to conceive, by force if necessary, a son and heir to his imammate. Al-Baghdadi advocates rape of captured women, and, by some accounts, is happy to give practical demonstrations. Neither has any notion of ethics and both betray an out-of-control bloodlust.

Both leaders are worshipped by their followers, and their orders, however perverse, are followed to the letter. Al-Baghdadi's followers move with the speed and fury of the intoxicated followers of Immortan.

ISIS has appeared from 'nowhere' in the sense that it has always been there. The theory of an Islamic state, ruled by the Shariah, the 'Islamic State' element of ISIS, has been around for the past six decades. It was the goal of most Wahhabi-inspired Islamic movements, some of which, such as Jamaat-e-Islami of Pakistan, we now see as 'moderate'. Admittedly, their notion of the Shariah would have been more classical and not as perverted and inhuman as that of ISIS. But while the 'Islamic State' of the Islamic movements was ultimately a national state, or an autonomous emirate like the one established by the Taliban in Afghanistan, ISIS aims at creating a severing caliphate that will ultimately be global in nature. Thus, ISIS has taken the theory of political Islam and the idea of an Islamic state to its logical conclusion.

But ISIS has also existed in practice since 1932: ISIS is Saudi Arabia.

The parallels between ISIS and Saudi Arabia are well illustrated by Rashid Moosagie, a madrassa-educated imam who left Cape Town with his wife and children to join

ISIS. Now by all accounts Moosagie was a sensible beard who shunned politics. So what attracted him to ISIS? The Islam he was taught, and was teaching, he says, was not true Islam. It was 'passive and submissive to infidel, secular laws, which is a kind of unbelief'. More specifically, it did not deal with 'the rules of jihad' and 'principles of war and slavery'. In a long and rambling letter written to his bewildered friends in South Africa, Moosagie explains what makes him 'happy here' and how he found 'what I missed all my life'. In the 'Dawla', he writes,

> You see full Sharia Law, absolutely NO kaafir court at all. All crime is strictly controlled with Sharia Law. Amongst the laws are:
>
> Execution for Irtidaad [apostasy], Sahr [black magic, witch-craft] and homosexuality
> Stoning for adultery
> Hands amputation for theft
> Flogging for Zina [sex between unmarried couples]
> Prison for Riba' [usury] and gambling [if discovered]
> Salaah [five times prayer] is enforced and all businesses to be closed upon Salaah times

No music allowed in homes or public areas

No wine and cigarettes

Full hijaab is enforced

No mixing of sexes in public

No cinemas, racecourses, banks, discos or clubs[10]

With a couple of exceptions, this is exactly what the Shariah law means in Saudi Arabia. And if the Saudi clerics had their way, they would totally ban music and have the banks closed too. ISIS, however, does have one important additional ingredient: millenarianism. The cult believes that we are living in the end times when the return of the Mahdi is imminent. There will be a great battle between the Mahdi and his opponent Dajjal (Antichrist). The prodigious battle will begin in the Syrian town of Dabiq, which is also the name of ISIS's English magazine. Or, as the deranged Moosagie puts it:

> Towards the hour Dajjal will appear and it is the greatest
> fitna [affliction] ever to surface on earth. The entire assem-
> bly of Ambiya alayi salaam [prophets] warned against this

---

10 http://thecentrestar.com/south-africas-second-letter-from-isis.

terrible fitna to appear, so know that it *is* going to be a
VERY GREAT FITNAH ... – *A Heaven and Hell*. Dajjal will come along and present this 'jannah and jahannum'
[paradise and hell] and everyone will opt for his 'jannah'.
Everyone will be commanding each other to choose his
'jannah' and NEVER to go towards his hell. It is absolutely
absurd to choose the hell of Dajjal. Despite all odds, a true
believer will opt for Dajjal's hell and this action will stir the
emotions of everyone – they will become furious, rebuke
and even fight with him for making such an 'outrageous
and despicable' decision. But the believer will insist to jump
into Dajjal's hell in true obedience to Nabie Salallahu Alayhi
Wasllam [the Prophet] who had forewarned the ummah
and instructed them to choose the hell of Dajjal as it will
in reality be a heaven. And those who opted for his heaven
will in realty [*sic*] have chosen Hell.

Much of this millenarianism is based on dubious and
fabricated traditions of the Prophet, who was a man
of reasoned thought, not inclined to irrational notions
about the future. But these traditions, and the Mahdi,
or the imam in occultation, as I mentioned earlier, are
a cornerstone of mainstream Shia theology. Indeed, the

former President of Iran Mahmoud Ahmadinejad was so obsessed by apocalyptic concerns that he predicted the Mahdi's arrival in a speech to the UN, and organised regular conferences to 'prepare for the arrival'. I was invited to speak at one; I declined politely and regretfully. ISIS, however, has added a new twist to this mythology: while the orthodox Shia wait passively and patiently for the end of days and the arrival of the Mahdi, ISIS wants to hasten the process and propagates the belief that its activities, seen by the world as 'outrageous and despicable', will speed up his return.

The parallels between ISIS and Saudi Arabia are stark. The Salafi-jihadis of ISIS subscribe to Wahhabism, the official state creed of Saudi Arabia. Just like the clerics in Saudi Arabia, ISIS rejects any interpretation of scriptural sources. Most of the leaders of the terrorist organisations learned their Salafism at the kingdom's universities or Saudi-backed madrassas. The Palestinian scholar Abdullah Yusuf Azam, known as 'the Father of Global Jihad', was a lecturer, during the '70s, at the King Abdulaziz University in Jeddah, where Osama bin Laden was one of his students. (I was there too, but in a different capacity.) Many of the early jihadis came from Palestinian refugee camps in Lebanon and Jordan where students were recruited, given scholarships and then transferred to Saudi institutions to be indoctrinated in Wahhabism and Salafism. The takfiri madrassas in Pakistan were established, funded and sometimes even managed by the Saudis; the students were frequently enrolled for postgraduate studies in Saudi universities. Indeed, most of the leading Salafis in Britain, Europe and most of the Muslim world have studied in Saudi Arabia and have received subsidies from the kingdom. The Salafi imams in numerous mosques in Britain are Saudi graduates, as are the imams of mosques funded by the Saudis throughout the world.

Thus, the seeds of ISIS have long antecedents. The story of the rise of Saudi Wahhabism is much like the story of Dave, the protagonist of Stephen Collins's wonderful graphic novel *The Gigantic Beard That Was Evil*.[11] Dave lives on a rather clean and sensible place, where not everything makes sense but people struggle to discover the meaning of life, called the Island of Here. Then one day, he wakes up to feel a 'roaring black fire climbing up through his face' as his beard appears from nowhere.

---

11 Jonathan Cape, London, 2013.

It is an extraordinary beard from a place far, far beyond the tidy and reasonably rational abode of Dave. And it grips Dave in a suffocating embrace. It grows and grows just as Wahhabism and Salafism have spread and spread. Dave trims his beard all night, hoping to bring it down to manageable proportions, but it is back at sunrise to its mammoth and monolithic self. Soon it spreads everywhere and becomes a petrifying spectacle. In the shape of ISIS, we are confronted with the terrifying hegemonic manifestation of Saudi Wahhabism and Salafism. As the Saudi clerics will readily tell you: it is the will of God.

Going to Syria

But why would anyone, particularly young people from Britain, want to join ISIS? The reasons, as my friend Sadakat Kadri, the human rights lawyer and author of *Heaven on Earth: A Journey Through Sharia Law*, suggested in *The Guardian* recently, are varied and complex. Some indeed go as an Islamic duty, but 'devotedness alone explains little'. The British recruits to ISIS 'all lived in deeply traditional communities, and though such places nurture some insular forms of behaviour, the abandonment of husbands and suicidal murder aren't among them'. They are 'maladjusted misfits: estranged from co-religionists rather than bound to them', who seek identity and belonging. ISIS provides them with a group identity of belonging to a gung-ho gang. Women are attracted for similar reasons: the 'eagerness among good Muslim girls to hook up with bad jihadi boys is a strong part of the group's appeal.'[12]

There is also an element of thrill seeking. The prospect of handling a machine gun or riding a tank like the stoned followers of Immortan Joe has a certain attraction for bored, maladjusted young British Muslim men. The very experience of communal combat, with imagined echoes of early warriors of Islam, and complete with the buzz of chants of 'Allah O'Akbar', orchestrated hatred, and blood, guts and brutal deaths, would probably be the high point of the disturbed and disillusioned lives of the recruits. Some romanticism is also involved in the very idea of going out to a distant war to fight against injustice and help a beleaguered community. More educated recruits to ISIS probably rationalise their actions as defensive jihad, against an enemy that has shredded Iraq, destroyed Afghanistan,

---

12 Sadakat Kadri, 'Rebellion, escape and the grim lure of Isis', *The Guardian*, 18 June 2015.

destabilised Pakistan and has a propensity to support and prop up dictators. They would ask: Why is it legitimate for the West to have weapons but illegitimate for Muslims to arm themselves? Why is it that Israel can have nuclear capability but Iran cannot? Why is it that the Saudis can be equipped with the latest weaponry but the Hutis and other groups fighting against them in Yemen, or those fighting against the Assad regime in Syria, are denied the means to fight and defend themselves? ISIS presents an opportunity for payback for such hypocritical policies.

Indeed, the more educated ISIS recruits are following a well-established British tradition. For example, in the late 1930s, a number of young British men, including George Orwell and Arthur Koestler, joined the Brigades to fight in the Spanish Civil War. They were misguided, as we later discovered, but their motives were honourable. As the highly regarded *Independent* columnist Boyd Tonkin points out:

> 'Objectively', to use that favourite bargaining chip of 1930s political argument, British and other volunteers may have helped the broader interests of a far-from-benign Soviet policy. Subjectively, save for an atypical handful of true

ideologues, they generally took up arms for liberty and in solidarity with a threatened people. Any neutral observer might imagine that their trajectory – fully documented in memoirs, interviews, films and histories – should have guided official reactions when young British men again began to journey overseas to help, and perhaps to fight. For in Syria, just as in Spain, the border between humanitarian assistance and military combat has turned out to be distinctly porous.[13]

What is definitely not porous is the education the jihadis have received. Takfiri jihadis are not ill or uneducated, although the converts tend to be – such as Sally-Anne Jones, one of the main recruiters for ISIS, who now faces UN sanctions over links with the organisation. She worked as a saleswoman and make-up artist and lived largely on benefits. But her fellow British jihadist Nasser Muthana, also facing UN sanctions, is a medical student; the current leader of al-Qaida, Ayman al-Zawahiri, is a qualified surgeon. The former leader, Osama bin Laden, was an engineer. The leader of the pack who committed

---

13 Boyd Tonkin, 'Volunteers and Terrorists', *Critical Muslim 11: Syria*, edited by Ziauddin Sardar and Robin Yassin-Kassab, Hurst, London, 2014, p. 126.

the 9/11 atrocity, Mohamed Atta, was an engineer. In fact, an exceptionally high percentage of jihadis and ISIS recruits, including British Muslims, come from engineering, medical or IT backgrounds. The link between takfiri jihadis and engineering can be seen everywhere, say Diego Gambetta and Steffen Hertog in 'Engineers of Jihad', a working paper published by the Department of Sociology of Oxford University.

Two of the three men who in 1987 founded Lashkar e-Toiba, a Sunni fundamentalist Pakistani group which fights against India's sovereignty over the State of Jammu and Kashmir, were professors at the University of Engineering and Technology of Lahore. While appealing to madrasa students and the disenfranchised, in South East Asia Jamaa Islamiya also recruited 'many technical faculty members, including architects, engineers, geophysicists, chemists, and robotics engineers', and the three leading suspects in the September 2004 bombing of the Australian Embassy in Jakarta have an engineering background.[14]

---

14 Diego Gambetta and Steffen Hertog, 'Engineers of Jihad', Sociology Working Papers 2007–10, Department of Sociology, Oxford University, pp. 4–5.

In 'Immunising the Mind', a study for the British Council, Martin Rose reaches a similar conclusion. Engineers, he says, 'seem to have left fingerprints all over the Islamist "violent extremism enterprise"'.[15] Even more revealing, suggests Rose, is the almost total absence of students of politics, sociology, history and philosophy – that is, social sciences and humanities. There is a good reason for this. Unlike the sixth formers of Belle Vue Girls' School, science, engineering and medical students are not taught critical reasoning and are seldom encouraged to ask searching questions. This is true even in Britain, where we pride ourselves at the excellence of our technical and medical courses. 'The manner in which US and European universities teach medicine', write Stephen Schwartz and his co-authors in 'Scientific Training and Radical Islam', 'is damaging to the ability of young medical students to think critically on a broader canvas'.[16] Ditto for science and engineering. There is now ample evidence to show that science, engineering and medical studies encourage binary understanding of correct and

---

15 Martin Rose, 'Immunising the mind: how can education reform contribute to neutralising violent extremism?', British Council, London, 2015, p. 10.

16 Stephen Schwartz, 'Scientific Training and Radical Islam', *Middle Eastern Quarterly*, Volume 15, No. 2 (spring 2008), pp. 3–11, unpaginated.

incorrect and of right and wrong. No attempts are made to explore social and ethical issues, or to inspire critical thought and questions. Thus ambiguity is suppressed, and certainty about facts and techniques is enforced – the traits that appeal to the Salafi and takfiri worldview.

But it is not just the jihadis who eschew ambiguity and uncertainty. This is also a major attribute of Islamic orthodoxy, where doubt is banned, criticism is seen as a sign of unbelief, and questioning is regarded as akin to rebellion and hence apostasy. Which brings us back to Rashid Moosagie. My friend the theologian Ebrahim Moosa, who teaches at University of Notre Dame, studied at the Deoband seminary in India with Moosagie. At Deoband, says Moosa, Moosagie hated politics and thought that the tradition of piety and poring over texts that are better forgotten was the best approach to studying Islam. So imagine Moosa's surprise at Moosagie's radical turn. 'I was very confused', writes Moosa in a *Washington Post* article, to learn that he 'immigrated to Syria and joined the Islamic State' and now 'claims it is theologically mandatory for a Muslim to migrate to a land where God's law is applied'. 'How could this have happened?' The answer, Moosa says, is that

Islamic orthodoxy, which controls mosques and institutions worldwide, is out of step with the world in which the majority of Muslims live. In few places is orthodox Islam independent of the state; it is often a political tool used by authoritarian regimes, which explains why the Muslim intelligentsia does not respect it. Its hallmark is archaism in theology and ethics, and its reach covers most of the global community of faith. Once a robust intellectual tradition, today Islamic orthodoxy is in serious need of a makeover. Mainstream theologians who cater to the majority of lay Muslims, both Sunni and Shiite, are unable to address such critical moral and theological challenges as evolution, gender and sexuality, or the role and meaning of sharia in a modern nation. That's because theological education is steeped in ancient texts with little attention to reinterpretation.[17]

Islamic orthodoxy

A great deal of the blame for the rise of ISIS, enticing young men and women to 'the caliphate', and the general malaise throughout the Muslim world has to be laid

---

17 Ebrahim Moosa, 'My madrassa classmate hated politics. Then he joined the Islamic state', *Washington Post*, 21 August 2015.

at the doorstep of Islamic orthodoxy. Indeed, it seems to me, that far from challenging Wahhabism, Islamic orthodoxy has in fact infused itself with Wahhabism – so now Wahhabism and Islamic orthodoxy have become one and the same thing. Whatever Moosagie learned from the madrassa in Deoband, he did not learn how to ask questions, or to engage his own conscience with the ethical issues of our time – he was taught to accept and obey. Which is exactly what he does when he is told by the takfiri-Salafists of ISIS that they represent the true path and that all other varieties of Islam are 'totally, totally, away from Islam', as he puts it.

A major problem with the 'traditional communities' that the human rights lawyer Sadakat Kadri talks about is that they also emphasise blind following (*taqlid*) and discourage all questioning and criticism of religious matters. Much of this mindless, unseeing tradition is propagated through the madrassa system. It is not surprising that the kind of jihadism we see in ISIS has its origins in the madrassas: the Taliban, as their name suggests, are literally the students of madrassas, as are the Shabab (youth) of Somalia, as are Nigeria's Boko Haram, whose name actually denounces all forms of education accept madrassa education. In Britain, we have numerous unregulated madrassas, usually with the august title of Dar-al-Uloom (House of Knowledge), which are teaching our young to be dogmatic, unquestioning and literalist. The emphasis in these schools is on memorisation and correct pronounce-ment, not on understanding, questioning or engaging with what they read. Two teachers from one such madrassa in Birmingham were recently jailed for a year for brutally beating a young boy with a stick for 'failing to read the Qur'an accurately'.[18] Such punishments are not unusual in madrasas in the Muslim world.

Islamic orthodoxy has made a series of category mis-takes that have now come back to haunt Muslims. Prime amongst these is the elevation of the Shariah to the level of the divine, with the consequent removal of agency from the believers, and the equation of Islam with the state. As such, most Muslims consider that the Shariah is man-dated by God and cannot be changed. It is, they believe, nothing more than the will of God. Yet there is nothing divine about the Shariah. The only thing that can legiti-mately be described as divine in Islam is the Qur'an. The

---

18 Adam Withnall, 'Teachers at Islamic school jailed for 12 months for beating 10-year-old pupil', *The Independent*, 10 September 2015.

Shariah is a human construction; an attempt to understand the will of God in a particular context. This is why the bulk of the Shariah actually consists of *fiqh* or jurisprudence, a collection of legal opinions of classical jurists. The very terms Shariah and *fiqh* did not exist in Islamic history before the Abbasid period, when it was actually formulated and codified.

When the Shariah was codified during the ninth century, it incorporated three vital aspects of Muslim society of the Abbasid period. At that juncture, Muslim history was in its expansionist phase, and the Shariah incorporated the logic of Muslim imperialism of that time. The rulings on apostasy, for example, derive not from the Qur'an but from this logic. Moreover, the world was simpler than it is today and could easily be divided into black and white: hence, the division of the world into *Dar al-Islam* and *Dar al-Harb* – the abode of Islam and the abode of war. Furthermore, the social customs of the period, such as slavery and gender relations, as well as obnoxious Arab customs, became an integral part of the Shariah. Now, all orthodox Muslims believe in the Shariah, and some would indeed defend this dangerously obsolete body of law or, as Moosa puts it, 'sharia-in-formaldehyde', with their life.

'Ordinary clerics are reluctant to replace the medieval rulings on blasphemy, apostasy and captives with new interpretations of Islamic law based on current realities. So a credible and sophisticated narrative of Islam remains out of the reach of most Muslims,' says Moosa.

In the absence of a 'sophisticated narrative of Islam', almost anything can be justified in the name of the Shariah – summary justice, beheadings, rape, slavery, forced conversion, war, misogyny, chauvinism, xenophobia and even fascism. And if a justification cannot be found in the Shariah then there is always recourse to manufactured hadith or traditions of the Prophet. The authentic traditions of the Prophet are relatively few in number – not more than a couple of thousand. But there are hundreds of thousands, if not millions, of dubious, fabricated, politically motivated and plainly daft sayings out there that are attributed to the Prophet Muhammad.

Many can be found in dubious, but reverential, collections. Islamic orthodoxy, because it emphasises reverence rather than critical engagement, has kept silence at this spectacle. While insulting the Prophet is regarded as blasphemy, which carries a death penalty in certain countries, quoting or using a dubious hadith that insults the Prophet's intelligence and integrity is a normal everyday occurrence. The whole body of apocalyptic hadith belongs to this category. Consider, for example, the hadith used by ISIS to entice recruits. These suggest that the Prophet was heard giving glad tidings to Syria (Sham) because 'the angels of Allah have rested their wings upon the Sham'. Another one reports that the Prophet said: 'I saw a pillar of the book was taken from underneath my pillow and I looked and it was an extending light directed toward Sham. Verily al-iman (the faith), at the time of fitna (turmoil) is in Sham.' Why has Allah chosen Sham for his angelic blessings, one may ask, and left the rest of Muslimkind in the lurch? And why would the Prophet, a man who emphasised thought and knowledge, and who rejected miracles and paranormal explanations, utter such words? No one bothers to ask.

But it is not just the dubious collections that are problematic. Even the two 'authentic' hadith collections that hundreds of millions of Muslims refer to daily contain examples confounding rationality. If, for example, we are to take certain 'authentic' hadith – that is, words actually spoken by the Prophet himself – in the canonical collection known as *Sahih al-Bukhari* then what are we to make of a string of rather irrational hadith to be found there? Consider: 'The sun rises between the two antlers of Satan' (*Sahih al-Bukhari* 2:134); or 'Do you ever see an animal born with deformed organs?' (*Sahih al-Bukhari* 1:525). Could the same Prophet who insisted that a solar eclipse coinciding with the death of his son was purely accidental and had nothing to do with heavenly intervention utter such words? Or what are we to make of the observation: 'The (Exalted) Messenger used to visit all nine of his wives every night' (*Sahih al-Bukhari*, Book of Nikah 3:52)? How could any man, no matter how close to the Prophet, have known this? And how could any man do this, particularly when we are told elsewhere in the same collection that he used to pray all night, so much so that his feet swelled? Or take the 'authentic' apocalyptic tradition much quoted by the followers of ISIS:

Abu Huraira reported Allah's Messenger (may peace be upon him) as saying: The Last Hour would not come until the Romans would land at al-A'maq or in Dabiq. An army consisting of the best (soldiers) of the people of the earth at that time will come from Medina (to counteract them). When they will arrange themselves in ranks, the Romans would say: Do not stand between us and those (Muslims) who took prisoners from amongst us. Let us fight with them; and the Muslims would say: Nay, by Allah, we would never get aside from you and from our brethren that you may fight them. They will then fight and a third (part) of the army would run away, whom Allah will never forgive. A third (part of the army). which would be constituted of excellent martyrs in Allah's eye, would be killed and the third who would never be put to trial would win and they would be conquerors of Constantinople. And as they would be busy in distributing the spoils of war (amongst themselves) after hanging their swords by the olive trees, the Satan would cry: the dajjal has taken your place among your family. They would then come out, but it would be of no avail. And when they would come to Syria, he would come out while they would be still preparing themselves for battle drawing up the ranks. Certainly, the time of prayer shall come and then Jesus (peace be upon him) son of Mary would descend and would lead them in prayer. When the enemy of Allah would see him, it would (disappear) just as the salt dissolves itself in water and if he (Jesus) were not to confront them at all, even then it would dissolve completely, but

Allah would kill them by his hand and he would show
them their blood on his lance (the lance of Jesus Christ).
(*Sahih Muslim*, 41:6924)

Nothing about this hadith actually makes sense: the
Romans are long gone, Constantinople has long been
conquered, no one fights with swords any more, Medina
hardly boasts the best soldiers of Allah, and the whole
narrative is totally out of character of the Prophet. Yet
pious Muslims everywhere take all this as absolute truth
because Islamic orthodoxy has failed to critically engage
with hadith collections and sift sense from nonsense.

The elevation of the Shariah and manufactured hadith
to the divine level has had a catastrophic effect on Muslims: the believers themselves have no agency. The will of
God has been made explicit in the Shariah and (invented)
traditions of the Prophet. All the Muslims have to do
is accept and obey – no matter how barbaric or absurd
the injunctions. The vast majority of Muslims, including highly educated ones, have become passive receivers
of obscurantist dogma, often presented as 'knowledge',
rather than active seekers after truth. And if they are educated in madrassas, or have a mindless degree in science,

engineering or medicine, they become empty vessels into which anything, however toxic, can be poured.

Thus, Islamic orthodoxy itself is now the biggest problem facing Muslims. It does not offer, as Moosa notes, 'a humane alternative'. Much of what ISIS propagates is also embraced by fundamentalist orthodox Muslims. The problem of dehumanised, perverted interpretations stems from a particular ossified Islamic tradition that has become dominant.

But the solution to the problem of all varieties of fundamentalism can also be found in Islamic tradition. For that we have to look towards the great critical and humanist tradition of Islam. The sixth formers at Belle Vue Girls' School knew this. That's why they asked me: 'Can you talk about the history and role of freethinking in Islam?'

'Yes, I can,' I replied. But we have to change gear and take a tour of early Islamic history.

Part II

What I know

ISLAMIC HISTORY IS full of critical voices and free-thinkers who provide us with a totally different take on Islam. This rich and diverse history goes right back to the formative phase of Islam. Those who believe that Muslims can't think may be surprised to discover that it was the Muslims who lived during the eighth to twelfth centuries who taught the West how to think.

The rational tradition of Islam derives its inspiration from the fundamental sources of Islam – the Qur'an and the actions and sayings of the Prophet Muhammad.

The emphasis the Qur'an gives to reasoning and critical thought is not widely recognised. The Sacred Text is saturated with references to reflection, criticism, learning, education, observation and the use of reason. Indeed, the very essence of the Qur'an, and hence of Islam, is summed up in the first verse of the Qur'an revealed to the Prophet Muhammad on the fateful night of 27 Ramadan 611:

> Read: In the Name of thy Lord who created,
> Created Man of a blood-clot.
> Read: And thy Lord is the Most Generous
> Who taught by the Pen
> Taught Man, that he knew not. (96:1–5)

What one is exhorted to read are the 'signs of God', which are manifest both in the revelation and in the material world. The Qur'an presents the cosmos as a 'text' that can be read, explored and understood with the use of reason: 'in the alternation of night and day, in the rain God provides, sending it down from the sky and reviving the dead earth with it, and in His shifting of winds there are signs for those who use their reason' (45:5). Thus, reason is the path to salvation: 'And they shall say, had we but listened or used reason, we would not be among the inmates of the burning fire' (67:10); reason is not something you set aside to have faith, it is the means to attaining faith, a tool of discovery and an instrument for getting close to God. 'The Pen', which has the most exalted place in Islam, is a metaphor for thought, reflection, criticism, the study of nature, the material world and general pursuit of knowledge. The Qur'an makes a distinction between 'those who have knowledge and those who have no knowledge' (39:9); and repeatedly asks the believers to think for themselves and study the signs of nature.

The Prophetic traditions supplement these teachings of the Qur'an. 'The ink of the scholar', the Prophet is reported to have said, 'is more sacred than the blood of the martyr.' He also said: 'Seek knowledge from the cradle to the grave'; 'An hour's study of nature is better than a year's adoration'; 'To listen to the words of the learned and to instil unto others the lessons of knowledge is better than religious exercise'; and 'Acquire knowledge: it enables its possessor to distinguish right from the wrong; it lights the way to Heaven; it is our friend in the desert, our society in solitude, our companion when friendless; it guides us to happiness; it sustains us in misery; it is an ornament among friends and an armour against enemies.'

The critical and freethinking tradition of Islam is based on these teachings. It began just over a hundred years after the death of the Prophet. During this period, there was no such thing as the Shariah, nor indeed was there an authentic collection of hadith. A century would pass before the first and most authentic collection, *Sahih al-Bukhari*, would emerge, and another century would pass after that before the Shariah would be codified. Grandchildren of the companions of the Prophet were still alive. Some of them, the story goes, were sitting in a mosque in Basra, Iraq, listening to a lecture by Hasan al-Basri (642–728). A scholar and theologian, al-Basri was highly respected, not least because he was brought up in the house of the Prophet's wife Umm Salama. He knew many companions of the Prophet and was famous for his austerity and piety. Amongst the students listening attentively to his lecture, sitting in a circle around him, were two young thinkers: Wasil ibn Ata (700–748) and Amr ibn Ubayd (d. 762). When al-Basri finished his lecture, Wasil asked him: is a person who has committed a sin a believer or an unbeliever? After a pause, al-Basri replied that he remains a believer. But, Wasil shot back, there is a third option: he is neither a believer nor an unbeliever, a position between two positions. Al-Basri was not particularly happy either with the third option or with Wasil's insubordination.

Now, both the question and the answer have a context. During the eighth century, the Kharjites, whom we met in Part I, were still around. They were ever ready to declare those who had committed a sin unbelievers and apostates who could therefore be killed. So al-Basri was being liberal and accommodating in his reply. Wasil, Amr and their fellow freethinkers had another concern. A great deal of what they were being taught was based on arguments from authority, which, they rightly deduced, can lead to political tyranny. They were being asked to blindly follow their forefathers. It is not that they did not trust their forefathers, or regarded them as irrational, or thought they were wrong. Their position was based on the verses of the Qur'an that ask the believers to question the ways and authority of their forefathers who sometimes 'do not know' and 'are only guessing': 'We saw our fathers following this tradition; we are guided by their footsteps' (43:22–23). Hasan al-Basri's freethinking students also thought that true knowledge comes from the clash of arguments.

Thus, the teacher and some of his students had a dispute.

It is interesting to note that the Qur'an often uses 'reason' in juxtaposition with 'listening' (as in 67:10, quoted above). Every reasoned argument has a counter-argument. While understanding comes from reasoning, it does not come from reasoning alone. We are also required to listen to the counter-argument and take it into consideration in our reasoning process. But al-Basri was in no mood to listen. As a result, Wasil and Amr, along with a few other students, withdrew from al-Basri's circle. The professor then announced to the remaining students that 'Wasil has withdrawn from us'. Historical accounts of this story vary slightly – some suggest that it was Amr who withdrew and not Wasil, others suggest that the withdrawal did not take place during the lecture but much later – but the overall gist of the story is the same.

The Mutazilites

The followers of Wasil and Amr came to be known as the Mutazilites – 'those who have withdrawn'. The movement they established, belonging to Sunni Islam, argued that Islamic theology should be based on reason and rational thought. Their overall position was based on five principles: God's justice, God's unity, the 'intermediate position' between two extremes (Wasil's third option), God's irreversible threats and promises, and God's commanding what is right and prohibiting what is wrong. These principles amounted to responses to their various rivals. These rivals included the literalists, who saw everything in black and white; the determinists, who believed in predestination and argued against free will; and the traditionalists, who relied excessively on the hadith. While reason played a vital part in Mutazila thought, it was much more than straightforward logical deduction. Reasoning had to lead to salvation and, as such, the question of 'how' a goal is achieved had to be considered with 'why' it is sought in the first place and whether it 'ought' to be pursued at all. But the Mutazila were not just rationalists: they were also humanists. They believed in free will and human agency – both to interpret the sacred sources and to shape the material world – and in freedom and progress based on evidence, empiricism and critical thinking. Amongst them were certain thinkers we would nowadays describe as 'secular humanists', but most were strong believers in God. And they were totally devoted to social justice.

There were three aspects of the moral philosophy of

the Mutazila that were deeply problematic for the wider community of Muslim scholars and thinkers. The first was related to their notion of divine justice. The Mutazila argued that the conventional, traditionalist position that whatever God commands is intrinsically good and what He forbids is inherently wrong makes a mockery of divine justice. It reduces human beings into automata with little to do but follow God's commands – or, more appropriately, what certain people think is the will of God and wish to impose on others. Rather, they argued, human beings should be able to rationally determine what is right and what is wrong and then freely choose their actions.

The second controversial aspect was the argument that only God's essence is eternal. When we think of God, they suggested, we think of Him in human terms; we can do nothing else. We think of Him as a Just and Merciful God, an Omnipresent and Omnipotent God, somewhere in the Heavens. But these are human notions based on our limited capability – they are not the same as God and cannot be eternal.

The third problem arose from their argument that the Qur'an, the Word of God, was created, that the revelation to Muhammad was an event in history and thus had a historical context. This had a particular theological significance: it meant that the Qur'an had to be interpreted in the light of history; its verses could only be understood by examining the social and cultural context within which they were revealed. As such, not everything in the Qur'an had universal validity. Some of its content was very specific and directed towards the historic community it was guiding during the life of the Prophet.

These problems with the moral philosophy of the Mutazila were further aggravated when they wholeheartedly embraced ancient Greek philosophy. By the middle of the ninth century, peripatetic philosophy was well established in Muslim civilisation and the Mutazila were amongst its leading proponents. The most noted philosopher of the period was another inhabitant of Basra: the polymath, mathematician and musical theorist al-Kindi (801–873), seen as the father of Islamic philosophy. Al-Kindi sought to show that philosophy and theology, or reason and revelation, are compatible and take us to the same conclusions. This led the detractors of the Mutazila to accuse them of relying on external sources, and giving absolute authority, which rightfully belonged to the Qur'an and the Prophet, to Greek philosophy.

The differences between the Mutazila and their opponents led to an immense clash of ideas. It became one of the greatest intellectual battles of Islamic history, lasting several centuries. Both sides had intellectual giants arguing and fighting for their case. A particular outcome of this almighty collision of opposing ideas was the emergence of a culture of acquiring knowledge, writing, arguing for one's particular position, and of general debate and discussion, to which all sides contributed. This culture was anchored on the *adab* (literally, etiquette) movement of classical Islam, which was concerned both with the techniques of intellectual discourse and with the etiquette of being human. Muslim civilisation developed a sophisticated system of teaching and learning that involved not just institutions such as the university, with its faculties of law, theology, medicine and natural philosophy, but also an elaborate method of instruction including work–study courses, a curriculum that included grammar, rhetoric, poetry, history, medicine and moral philosophy, and mechanisms for the formation of a humanist culture such as academic associations, literary circles, clubs and other coteries that sustain intellectuals and the literati. An immense body of work known as *adab* literature was produced to promote humanism.[19] The term *adab* was itself immensely debated, different definitions giving emphasis to religious, philological, artistic and philosophical aspects of what it means to be a cultured human being. At the epicentre of *adab* was the book: a great deal of thought and energy was given to how the book should be written, read, classified and arranged in a library; how the text itself should be treated, examined and critiqued; and how the knowledge contained in the book should be transmitted to the next generation. It was a culture that was passionate about books, fascinated with different ideas and opinions contained in the books, and awash with books.

The *adab* movement and Mutazila free thought reigned supreme from the eighth to the twelfth century. The Mutazila included all sort of characters, theologians, scientists, poets, mystics and libertarians. The greatest philosophers of Muslim civilisation were largely Mutazilites. These included al-Kindi; al-Farabi (d. 950), known after Aristotle as 'the Second Teacher' and author of *The Perfect State*; Ibn Sina (980–1037), encyclopaedist, physician, psychologist, author of the standard text *Canon of Medicine* (used

---

19 See George Makdisi, *The Rise of Humanism in Classical Islam and the Christian West*, Edinburgh University Press, 1990.

in medical training in Islam and the West till the seventeenth century), master and commentator on and corrector of Aristotle, described by the noted historian of science, George Sarton, as 'the most famous scientist of Islam and one of the most famous of all races, places and times';[20] and Ibn Rushd (1126–98), physician, scientist, linguist, theologian and 'The Commentator' on Aristotle and Plato and known as 'the greatest Muslim philosopher of the West'.

Al-Farabi, who established his own school of early Islamic philosophy, was as much concerned with metaphysics as with methodology. For him, the human intellect came in three varieties: the active intellect, Plato's world of ideas; the potential intellect, the inherent capacity to acquire eternal truths; and the acquired intellect, developed through learning. The inhabitants of a good city, being endowed with intellect, he argued, should be able to rise above material obsessions, and behave justly towards one another, just as God demands. And the city itself should establish laws based on rational and philosophical thought that facilitate such behaviour. Al-Farabi himself lived a rather austere life and believed that happiness comes from

20 George Sarton, *Introduction to the History of Science*, Robert Krieger Publishing Company, New York, 1931, Volume 1, p. 721.

dissociation from material life and comfort, although, like the Sufis, the Muslim mystics, he did not advocate a solitary life devoted totally to the contemplation of God. Rather, true happiness or virtue could only be acquired while living a full life in busy, bustling cities.

Ibn Sina was deeply influenced by al-Farabi, although that influence did not extend to an austere life. His hedonistic lifestyle attracted much disapproval, and his pursuit of patronage sometimes got him into serious trouble. But this did not prevent him from working and writing prolifically. His major philosophical work is *Book of Healing*, an encyclopaedia of Islamic and Greek learning, from logic to mathematics, in the early Abbasid period. He devoted his considerable intellectual energies to philosophically describing the relationship between divine essence and being. Ibn Sina argued that existence cannot be derived from the essence of existing things. Existence precedes essence: because God exists, therefore He has an Essence. Ibn Sina attempted to solve the problem of evil by distinguishing between inherent and extraneous causes. Like al-Farabi, he believed in the unity of knowledge with logic at the apex, followed by physics, mathematics and metaphysics. Ibn Sina grew up in a household that belonged to the Ismaili sect but spent much of his later life distancing himself from the community. In his famous *Autobiography*, he claims to be a Sunni of the Hanafi school. None of which saved him from the vitriolic attacks of the orthodox theologians.

Many Mutazila thinkers were also scientists and men of medicine. The Basra-born al-Jahiz (776–868), for example, produced a seven-volume study called *The Book of Animals*, which comes close to what we would recognise as a theory of evolution by natural selection. Written within a specific genre of classical Muslim scholarship, *The Book of Animals* combines facts and speculations about animals with poetry, humorous anecdotes, philosophical conjectures, metaphysics, sociology, anthropology and verses from the Qur'an. Al-Jahiz, who suffered from eye defects and was known as 'goggle eyed', emphasises our interconnectedness to the natural world by constantly using the images of nets and webs; and his web of interdependencies foreshadows Darwin's vision of the 'entangled bank', the extended metaphor Darwin used to distil the key idea of natural selection.[21] Al-Jahiz, who

---

21 One of the best analyses of al-Jahiz's evolution thought is provided by Rebecca Stott, *Darwin's Ghosts*, Bloomsbury, London, 2013. See also, J. E. Montgomery, *Al-Jaziz: In Praise of Books*, Edinburgh University Press, 2013.

also recognised eco-systems in the natural world, argued that society needed freethinking to ensure it was a fit response to God's revelation of the Qur'an. He did not accept the views of others without question or see himself as an authority to be followed unquestioningly. His polemical and literary works were written as an invitation to critical thought, to challenge his own views, and demanded intensive scrutiny from the reader. Another Mutazila stalwart, Abu Bakr al-Razi (854–925), polymath, natural scientist and physician, wanted to take Muslim society beyond limited theological reasoning to scientific thought. He produced theoretical criticism of the body of inherited medical knowledge. Emphasising observational diagnosis and therapy, al-Razi focused on method and practice. His book *On Smallpox and Measles* is thought to be the first theoretical account of the diagnosis and treatment of these two diseases and the difference between their symptoms.

One of my favourite freethinkers of the period is the Persian polymath al-Biruni (973–1048). He was a freethinker, writes the historian of Islamic civilisation Bruce Lawrence, 'not only in his own epoch, but also across the ages, in all the annals of Islamic history extending to culture and religion as well as mathematics and astronomy'.[22] While acknowledging the truth of Islam, al-Biruni recognised that other religions too had legitimate claims to truth. He saw a common human element in the numerous religions and cultures he studied, and argued that cultures were related to each other. He sought to break down boundaries wherever he saw them, including the boundaries of different disciplines. We could move from discipline to discipline, he showed, provided we respect the method of each discipline. But no scientific answer, whether obtained through reason or experience, experimentation or dissertation, was considered by al-Biruni to be absolute. He was the most exact of scientists without being fooled into believing that the method of experimental sciences could lead him to eternal truths, or be applied to religion or the humanities. He used one method to determine the specific gravity of certain metals, another to study Indian culture, and yet another to write a history of religions. This is why, for al-Biruni, there is no single method for the pursuit of knowledge but rather *methods* for acquiring all types of knowledge, in accordance with the innate nature

---

22   Bruce Lawrence, 'Al-Biruni: Against the Grain', in *Critical Muslim 12: Dangerous Freethinkers*, edited by Ziauddin Sardar, Hurst, London, 2014, pp. 61–72.

of what is being studied and explored. The answers you get, argues al-Biruni, depend on the nature of the questions, the way the questions are formed, the area under study and the methods used.

He moved freely from discipline to discipline, making invaluable contributions, changing his questions and methods according to the dictates of inquiry. He studied Hinduism and yoga according to their own concepts and categories; his book *India* is regarded as a masterful study of comparative religion. Al-Biruni thought that his fellow Mutazila philosophers themselves did not always ask the right questions. In particular, he singled out Ibn Sina's reliance on Aristotelian physics, and began a correspondence with him. Why, he asked, did Ibn Sina continue to rely on Aristotle when 'it is possible to prove that some part of Aristotelian natural philosophy does not fit all the evidence, the entire system becomes suspect, its formulations unhinged'? Al-Biruni asks a series of questions on the nature of the planetary system, such as how do you explore weight in space and how does one determine whether heavenly spheres are heavy or light. One particular question was directly relevant to metaphysical inquiry: are there other worlds than the cosmos, as we know it from mathematical astronomy? For both Ibn Sina and Aristotle, the answer was no. But for al-Biruni there was always a third option: maybe. Though we cannot prove the existence of other worlds, neither can we disprove their existence, he argued. Al-Biruni taught me how to raise critical questions, and I would venture to suggest that he did the same for the entire Muslim civilisation. He saw criticism and free thought as something profound – a progressive ideal that seeks to liberate humanity from all variety of misery and authoritarianism. Including, one must add, the authority of free thought based on instrumental reason itself.

Many thinkers took advantage of the general cultural fluidity of the time to throw hazardous projectiles at orthodox, conservative thinking. One of the earliest sceptics was al-Rawandi (827–911), who was himself an accomplished theologian. Al-Rawandi started off as a Mutazilite thinker, but then rejected the Mutazila principles and became a Shia. The conversion turned out to be even more confining than the philosophy he wanted to leave behind. So he became a libertarian and took every opportunity to question Islamic orthodoxy. Can the Muslim paradise be pleasing to anyone but a rustic, he demanded to know.

And why did the heavenly host of avenging angels help Muhammad's army at the 624 Battle of Badr – a common belief amongst Muslims – while at the 625 Battle of Uhud they stood by as onlookers?

The celebrated Abbasid poet and atheist Abu Nawas (756–814), a companion to the Caliph Harun al-Rashid (763–809), and a character who makes several appearances in *Arabian Nights*, used his considerable wit to mock orthodox Islam and openly displayed his excesses – most notable in his wine-poems. The blind poet and philosopher Abul 'Ala al-Ma'arri (973–1057) denounced dogmatisms and superstition and looked at all religion with scepticism, seeking to correct 'what established religion took for God's criteria'. Al-Ma'arri's quest in life was to discover the meaning of life, but it was a quest that only brought him misery. Wisdom demands, he suggests, that believers and non-believers – impotent as they are – should be satisfied with their lot, devote their lives to reasoned contemplation and good works, and shun the pursuit of wealth and happiness:

> *The finest of time's gift is to forsake what is given;*
> *God extends a predatory hand to what He has provided.*

> *Better than a life of wealth is one of poverty; a monk's*
> *Garb is better than a king's fine clothes.*[23]

In pushing the boundaries of free thought, the mystics were not far behind the poets and philosophers. The most noted mystic of the Abbasid period is Mansur al-Hallaj (858–922). A giant of Sufism, he is regarded as a great spiritual poet. He had utter contempt for authority, disliked the norms and values of orthodox society, and immersed himself perpetually in the love of God. He preferred to preach to the poor in the suburbs of Baghdad, as well as to nomads, robbers, bandits and criminals. Al-Hallaj, who produced highly sophisticated theological and literary works, saw God everywhere and invoked Him constantly, eventually to fatal effect. His most famous public utterance is: '*Ana al-Haqq*' ('I am the Truth'), and in one of his mystical poems, delivered in public, he comes face to face with God:

> *I saw my Lord with the eye of the heart*
> *I asked, 'Who are You?'*
> *He replied, 'You.'*

---

23 Quoted by Roger Allen, *The Arabic Literary Heritage*, Cambridge University Press, 1998, p. 201.

Not surprising, the orthodox and pious folks found this a bit shocking. He was accused of heresy, and after a long investigation and drawn-out trial, al-Hallaj was executed. An elaborate mythology has developed around both his trial and his subsequent execution.[24]

The analytical free thought unleashed by the Mutazila had two registers, suggests Aziz al-Azmeh, a highly regarded Professor of Islamic History. 'One is unstructured, playful, often frivolous, jocular impiety and blasphemy, often associated with libertine individuals and milieus of the courtly and literary elite'; the other is 'high-minded, serious, systematic and theologically and philosophically engaged'.[25] From their different perspectives, the theologians, philosophers, poets and mystics arrived at common conclusions: organised religion is not necessary, religions contradict themselves and one another, and religions are full of dogma and rituals that are absurd and insulting to reason. Quite clearly, these are dangerous assertions for a society knee-deep in conservative theology.

---

24 See Robert Irwin, 'Al-Hallaj's Truth, Massignon's fiction', in *Critical Muslim 12: Dangerous Freethinkers*, edited by Ziauddin Sardar, Hurst, London, 2014, pp. 51–60.

25 Aziz Al-Azmeh, 'Abbasid Culture and the Universal History of Freethinking Humanism', in *Critical Muslim 12: Dangerous Freethinkers*, ibid., pp. 73–88.

Yet this was not a total rejection of God. It is just that these freethinkers preferred a belief in a supreme being based on reason. Or, as al-Azmeh put it, 'Underlying all this chaos and disturbance is a diffuse divinity of Deistic description, which might, under conditions never specified, be conducive to human improvement.' The Mutazila free thought was a missile aimed directly at the orthodoxy. Not surprisingly, the guardians of belief and custom took suitable action against free thought in general, and the Mutazila in particular.

The Asharites

The main opponents of the Mutazila emerged, during the tenth century, as a direct response to the rapid spread of their thought. It was a school of Sunni theology known as Asharite, named after its founder Abul Hasan al-Ashari (873/4–936). He too was from Basra, where he studied theology and philosophy under a prominent Mutazila teacher. Al-Ashari himself became a noted member of the Mutazila school till the age of forty, when he had a spiritual experience. Apparently, he saw the Prophet in a series of dreams. The Prophet told him to devote the rest of his life to promoting and championing the *sunnah*, the example and traditions of the Prophet. Al-Ashari emerged from the dream a reinvigorated man and launched a furious attack on his Mutazilite friends and colleagues, feverishly writing up to 300 books in the process. Al-Ashari, who was a theological rationalist, was immediately joined by those who preferred a more literal interpretation of the Qur'an and less philosophical, more concrete, humanised understanding of God. Amongst these were the staunch conservatives belonging to the Hanbali school of Islamic jurisprudence – now the principal school of law in Saudi Arabia.

The stakes were high, and the Asharites and Mutazilites attacked each other with all the intellectual acumen they could muster. Their arguments focused on a question that seems like theological hair splitting: was the Qur'an created or uncreated? But the fact is the Mutazili position allowed for greater freedom in the interpretation of the Qur'an, saw truth simultaneously as absolute and relative, promoted pluralism in belief and thought, and saw the world not as black and white but in much more nuanced shades of grey.

In the first instance, the battle was settled not through intellectual arguments but by the use of power. The

Mutazila received support from successive Abbasid caliphs, including al-Mamun (786–833), the son of Harun al-Rashid, and the founder of the House of Wisdom in Baghdad, where al-Kindi and other Mutazili philosophers worked. But caliphs are caliphs because they like to wield power. Mutazilism was established as the philosophy of the state by force rather than persuasion by the Abbasid Caliph al-Mamun. Theologians were persecuted in Baghdad for not being rational enough. 'The people of that time went so far', writes the thirteenth-century historian Marrakushi in his *History of the Maghreb*, 'as to condemn as an unbeliever anyone who appeared to be entering upon the sciences of theology', which were seen as 'vile'.[26] Hatred of theology and its theories was the norm. Al-Mamun introduced the Mihna, the 'testing' or 'trial', to force theologians to justify their positions on rational grounds. It led to the incarceration of the noted theologian and jurist Ahmad ibn Hanbal (780–855), founder of the Hanbali school of Islamic jurisprudence.

The 'ordeal' was ended by Caliph al-Mutawakkil (822–861). By now, the Asharites had gained considerable

---

ground. And al-Mutawakkil found it easy to outlaw the belief that the Qur'an was uncreated. But an even more serious blow to the Mutazila came in 1017, when another Abbasid caliph, al-Qadir (947–1031), issued a famous decree declaring that Mutazila were anti-orthodox, and banned them from teaching, discussing or otherwise propagating their ideas. The caliph, seeing them as contentious, not only banished them but also ordered the imams to curse them from the pulpit. A few years later, al-Qadir issued another decree that defined orthodoxy, known as the Qadiri creed. Its principal dogma was that 'the word of God is not created' and that it remains uncreated whether recited, written or heard. Anyone denying or disagreeing with this assertion, or questioning it in any way, was automatically an 'unbeliever whose blood is permissible to shed – should he refuse to repent of his error when called upon to do so'. Hence, Caliph al-Qadir declared unthinkable – what the Mutazila were trying to make thinkable.[27] Sunnism, as understood today, is the Qadiri creed all but in name.

The critics of the Mutazila – the Ashari, the Hanbalis,

---

27 Mohammed Arkoun, *The Unthought in Contemporary Islamic Thought*, Saqi Books, London, 2002, p. 13.

and theologians of other ilk – saw free thought as a threat to orthodox religion. But what free thought actually represented was not a threat to religion per se but to the existence of the religious state. It was essentially a rebellion against the use of religion to establish and support an authoritarian state. This is well illustrated by another resident of Basra, the author and thinker Ibn al-Muqaffa (d. 756). Renowned for his eloquence, he was an exceptionally talented prose stylist and translator. His translation of the Persian animal tales, *Kalila wa-Dimna*, is regarded as a masterpiece. His day job involved working as a secretary to various Umayyad governors; thus he had first-hand knowledge of how religion was used in politics to reinforce the structures of the state. His major works include *The Book of Courtly Etiquette*, a manual on decorum and civil behaviour for officials. Ibn al-Muqaffa was against religion that has become 'a political artefact in the hands of the sovereign manipulating the rough and credulous demos', a 'rank unreason belonging wholly to the reason of state'.[28] Naturally, the Abbasid caliphs did not look kindly towards such declarations. Indeed, the tone of a letter written by

28 Al-Azmeh, op cit.

Ibn al-Muqaffa to Caliph al-Mansur upset the monarch, and Ibn al-Muqaffa was executed.

However, executions, political suppression, banishment of critical thought, and declarations of heresy did not rid Muslim civilisation of Mutazila thinkers or their thought. While Asharism was becoming the main Sunni theological school in Baghdad, Mutazilism had found a new home in al-Andalus. Unlike Baghdad, al-Andalus was a pluralistic, multicultural, multi-religious society. Muslims arrived in Hispania, as it was then known, during the early eighth century. They settled in a region that was already religiously, culturally and ethnically diverse, with a tradition of scholarship, art, law and of questioning imperial authority. They married local women from Eastern and Western European backgrounds. It was in this society of 'mixed marriages' between Christians, Jews and Muslims that Abd al-Rahman, the founder of the Umayyad caliphate in Spain (756–1031), escaping the massacre of his clan in Damascus, established the first great Western city of Islam: Cordoba. Its international fame rested on 113,000 homes, twenty-one suburbs, seventy libraries and numerous bookshops, mosques and glorious palaces. It inspired awe and admiration because it was a heaven for thinkers, philosophers,

musicians and writers. Al-Andalus was home to great philosophers such as Ibn Rushd who rubbed shoulders with
evolutionary thinkers like Ibn Tufayl. Scientists such as
Abbas ibn Firnás, the Andalusian Leonardo, who invented
and manufactured many instruments, including a flying
machine, using which he crash-landed on Cordoba's main
street; and al-Zahrawi, considered 'the father of modern surgery', inventor of numerous surgical instruments
and author of a thirty-volume encyclopaedia of medical
practice, *Kitab al-Tasrif*, that served as a standard text in
Europe for five centuries. Feminist intellectuals such as
Ibn Hazm, the author of the love manual *The Ring of the
Dove*, which contains surprisingly vivid anecdotes; and
brilliant musicians and fashion icons like Ziryab, who is
credited with adding an extra string to the Oud, establishing beauty parlours for women, and introducing the idea
of a three-course meal that should be eaten properly, sitting down, on a well laid-out table, accompanied by fine
beverages that should only be drunk in crystal glasses.
As well as numerous artists, poets, architects and mystics
such as Ibn Arabi.

Moreover, women in al-Andalus, unlike in Baghdad,
had a great deal of freedom and were involved in most

aspects of public life. In fact, we can safely say that women in al-Andalus played a more active part, and accomplished more, than women in any other period of Muslim history. The counsel of female scholars, scientists and philosophers was actively sought, female poets held splendid poetry recitals, and women worked and walked freely in the public space – often without, we may add, the burden of hijab. The beautiful and gracious Umayyad princess Walladah, for example, organised and engaged in poetic contests and played host to poets and artists in her Cordoba home. She never married; and declared: 'By God, I am suited to great things, and proudly I walk, with head aloft.' The eloquent poetess Hafsah bint al-Hajja al-Rukuniya rejected the advances of the ruler of Granada and chose to marry a fellow poet. The writer and poet al-Abbadiyyah, who spoke several languages, rose from her humble slave background to become a recognised authority on poetics; she eventually married the ruler of Seville. Female writers and poets were as famous as their male counterparts; and even the male scholars and thinkers of al-Andalus, such as Ibn Hazm and Ibn Arabic, championed feminism. Indeed, there were so many prominent women in public life, from so many diverse backgrounds, that it was considered natural for them to be leaders. The only remaining issue was whether they could be Prophets as well. Ibn Hazm thought it was an issue 'on which we know of no debate except here in Cordoba and in our time'. The public opinion, Ibn Hazm tells us, was divided into three. First, those who denied that women can be Prophets and argued that it will be an intolerable innovation (*bida*) in religious affairs. Second, those who had no problem with the proposition and saw no theological reason why women could not be Prophets. Third, the don't knows, who also included those who were afraid to take part in such discussions. There was little doubt in Ibn Hazm's mind: 'We find no proof for those who claim that Prophethood is impossible for women,' he declared. After all, there are many female Prophets in the Qur'an, including Mary, mother of Jesus, and Sarah, the mother of Isaac. As far as al-Andalus was concerned, there was no limit to what women could do and achieve.

Al-Ghazali's attack

All this coming from the periphery to the centre in Baghdad must have sent shivers down the spines of Islamic orthodoxy. The man who took it upon himself to do something about it was theologian and jurist Al-Ghazali (1058–1111). After a wide-ranging education in theology, law and philosophy, and after publishing a string of books, Al-Ghazali landed the most prestigious chair of the time: he became professor at the Nizamiyya Academy in Baghdad. But then, as he tells us in his autobiography, *Deliverance from Error*, he had an intellectual and spiritual crisis: 'When I examined my knowledge, I found that none of it was certain except matters of sense perception and necessary truth.' He thus abandons the world, disposes of his wealth, makes arrangements for his family and sets off in a quest for truth as an ascetic. The truth he discovers is the philosophical theory of occasionalism: that is, causal events and interactions are not the products of other created events but of the will of God. Having arrived at the truth, and banished all doubt, Al-Ghazali sits down to write *The Incoherence of the Philosophers*, an attack on scepticism in general and the Mutazila in particular.

Al-Ghazali considered the Muslim society of his time to be deeply afflicted with social sickness, 'an epidemic among the multitude', as he calls it. The only cure was a 'moral therapy', a heavy dose of religious devotion and piety, or the will of God. Muslims, he suggested, were 'straying from the clear truth', influenced by those insistent 'upon fostering evil' and 'flattering ignorance'. All of those who are lured by 'the Satan', he tells us in *The Book of Knowledge*, 'see good as evil and evil as good, so that the science of religion has disappeared and the torch of true faith has been extinguished all over the world'.[29] His ire was especially directed towards a particular 'class of men' who have 'greater intelligence and insight' but 'have abandoned all the religious duties Islam imposes on its followers', 'defy the injunction of the Sacred Law', and 'indulge in diverse speculations'. These people, Al-Ghazali squawks, hold 'irresponsible views', have 'perverted minds', and 'must be branded with diabolical perversity and stupid contumacy'. These men were inspired by the 'intellectual power' of 'Socrates, Hippocrates, Plato, Aristotle'. They are 'the heretics of our time'.[30]

So Al-Ghazali brands the Mutazila as 'heretics' – the very people who laid the foundations of the Muslim

---

29 Al-Ghazali, *The Book of Knowledge*, translated by Nabih Amin Faris, Ashraf, Lahore, 1962, pp. 1–2.

30 All quotations, here and later, are from Al-Ghazali, *The Incoherence of the Philosophers*, translated by Sabih Ahmad Kamali, Pakistan Philosophical Congress, Lahore, 1963, pp. 1–3, 163–7, 176, 181 and 88.

civilisation, the beacons of thought and learning whose names are intrinsically linked to 'the Golden Age of Islam'. His criticism of philosophers comes in two parts. First, he accuses Muslim philosophers of taking a rather uncritical attitude to 'ancient masters'. The works of Plato and Aristotle are regarded as 'unquestionable', and their mathematics, logic and deductive methods are seen as 'the most profound' and used to repudiate 'the authority of religious law' and deny 'the positive contents of historical religions'. Second – and this is what really troubles him – their beliefs, or *aqidah*, are not correct. It is the sort of accusation that conservative Wahhabis, extremist Salafis and militant Talibans routinely throw at all those who disagree with them. But Al-Ghazali was far more sophisticated: using their own rhetoric and method, he took the battle to the philosophers themselves.

The Incoherence of the Philosophers is an angry book. It is full of the sort of name-calling and livid asides not usually associated with a work of philosophy. In the preface, Al-Ghazali tries to defend the practice of offering prayer during an eclipse on the authority of a tradition of the Prophet. The philosophers explained the solar and lunar eclipses in scientific terms, as natural phenomena, and rejected the idea of praying during an eclipse. Al-Ghazali acknowledges that 'these things have been established by astronomical and mathematical evidence which leaves no room for doubt'. Nevertheless, since the Prophet declared that 'when you see an eclipse you must seek refuge in the contemplation of God and in prayer', the eclipse prayer is obligatory. Then we move on to twenty 'theories' of the philosophers, such as their doctrine of the eternity of the world, their alleged denial of divine attributes, and their belief in the impossibility of departure from the natural course of events. Al-Ghazali sets out to demolish these theories one by one. Thirteen theories are found to be problematic. On three points (the assertion that the world is everlasting, the denial that God knows the particulars, and the denial of bodily resurrection in the Hereafter) he judges the philosophers to be totally outside Islam, *kafirs* (infidels) to boot. The other theories and assertions are seen as heretical.

By any intellectual standards, *The Incoherence of the Philosophers* is not a 'major assault' on philosophy, as it is commonly depicted, but a poor polemic, and an insulting one too. To actually point this out itself tantamount to heresy. Al-Ghazali is a giant figure of Muslim

PART II

civilisation, perhaps the most influential person in Islam after the Prophet. He casts an overwhelming shadow over most of what nowadays passes as theology in Islam. He is lionised, revered, described as 'the Proof of Islam', and has even been projected as a postmodern philosopher! In certain circles, criticism of Al-Ghazali is seen almost as a blasphemy. I should know: he was my guru during my troublesome youth; a copy of his *Book of Knowledge* was always on my bedside table. But whatever one thinks of Al-Ghazali, it cannot be denied that he was a stalwart of Islamic orthodoxy, which he sought to protect from the attacks, not to mention sarcasm and ridicule, of freethinkers – always a force to be reckoned with.

Al-Ghazali states the positions of the philosophers reasonably well, but his counter-arguments are trite and often quite irrational. A couple of examples should suffice. In Al-Ghazali's day, philosophers argued that the movement of heavenly bodies is due either to (1) the intrinsic nature of these bodies, such as the downward movement of a stone, which is an unconscious act; or (2) an outside force that moves the body, which will be conscious of the movement. Al-Ghazali counters with three arguments. First, 'the movement of Heaven may be supposed to be the result of the constraint exercised by another body which wills its movement, and causes it to revolve perpetually. This motive body may be neither a round body nor a circumference. So it will not be a heavenly body at all.' Second, the heavenly bodies move by the will of God. Third, the heavenly bodies are specifically designed to possess the attribute of movement. These arguments, asserts Al-Ghazali, cannot be disproved! To the philosopher's assertion that angels are 'immaterial beings' which do not exist in space or act upon bodies, and should be understood in an allegorical or metaphorical sense, Al-Ghazali replies: 'How will you disprove one who says God enables the Prophet to know the Hidden Things?' Or deny that 'he who has a dream comes to know the hidden things, because God, or one of his angels, enables him to know them'? This is not philosophy but the notions of a man who is determined to keep a closed mind on matters of science out of fear that the orthodox dogma would be undermined if rationality is taken too seriously.

It has to be said that Al-Ghazali is big on the supernatural, an area he calls 'subsidiary sciences'. He quite likes the fact that the philosophers promote inquiry into physical sciences such as mathematics, physics, astronomy and botany, but he is not too happy with their concept of causality, the assertion that every cause must have an effect. He is enraged, for example, at the fact that the philosophers laugh at the suggestion that – as a fabricated narration states – the Prophet split the moon. The philosophers rightly dismissed the tradition as nonsense. He is outraged that the philosophers deny that Moses's rod literally turned into a serpent. The philosophers argued that the Qur'anic story is an allegory; a refutation of the doubts of the unbelievers by the divine proof manifested at the hands of Moses. He is horrified that the philosophers refuse to believe in resurrection after death, a fundamental belief in Islam. The philosophers argued that the resurrection is a symbolic reference to death arising from ignorance and life emerging from knowledge.

Not everything can be explained by cause and effect, Al-Ghazali argued; and it is the job of 'subsidiary sciences' to explain things which exist beyond the domain of rationality. The reader is generously provided with a list of these 'subsidiary sciences', including astrology, dream interpretation, 'the talismanic art', 'the art of magic', alchemy, and 'physiognomy' – which 'infers moral character from physical appearance' (this science would no doubt locate me in an amoral universe).

The Al-Ghazali that emerges from *The Incoherence* is a literalist, anti-rational scholar who is keen to cast a critical eye on philosophy yet eager to accept dogma and belief, including miracles and irrational sayings uncritically attributed to the Prophet. His main goal is to show that such metaphysical doctrines as the world having a Creator, that two gods are impossible, or that the soul is a self-subsistent entity, cannot be proved by reason – which is an eminently reasonable thing to say. But he gets carried away and jettisons reason and 'intellectual inquiry' altogether from religion. The inductive leap to rejecting scientific inquiry per se is only natural: 'Let us give up the inquiry concerning "why" and "how much" and "what". For these things are beyond the power of men.' Today, this message is regularly broadcast by countless bearded clerics and mullahs on thousands of television stations and websites.

Al-Ghazali's anger is understandable. It was due partly to the Mihna, the Abbasid-era purge of literalist theologians; and partly to the fact that theology was seen in a negative light and the study of the Qur'an and traditions of the Prophet were in decline, although the Qadri creed was the official religion of the state. The learned, particularly in al-Andalus, preferred philosophy to theology. Those inclined towards religious thought opted for Sufism rather than orthodox theology. Al-Ghazali's own works were banned in the Maghreb and Andalusia. The Berber Almoravids, who controlled large parts of Spain and the Maghreb, did not take kindly to his theology. The Almoravid ruler Ali ibn Yusuf (r. 1106–42) ordered his books to be burnt, anyone found in possession of his books had their property confiscated, and he was even threatened with execution. So Al-Ghazali suffered for his beliefs.

But all that does not deter us from seeing his arguments as obscurantist, irrational and, frankly, extremist. As we learn from his autobiography, *Deliverance from Error*, Al-Ghazali moved from one extreme to another in his own life: from being a total sceptic to an enthusiastic believer who emphatically declared, 'Reason is false.' He supported the fanatic Almoravids even though they banned his books! And there is just too much piety and uncritical acceptance of dogma in his work for an inquiring mind to take. Yet, Al-Ghazali's attack on philosophy and free thought is regarded as a fatal blow to the Mutazila.

Ibn Rushd's defence

The counter-attack came from al-Andalus; and the man who took upon himself to reply to Al-Ghazali was Ibn Rushd (1126–98). He was born in Cordoba to a distinguished family of jurists fifteen years after the death of Al-Ghazali. He studied jurisprudence, theology, linguistics, medicine and philosophy under distinguished scholars of the period. Al-Ghazali acolytes often dismiss Ibn Rushd as not very spiritual or particularly pious – a common, rather vulgar, trait of conservative Muslim scholars enthralled to the dogmatism of Islamic theology. So it is worth making a quick comparison of the two thinkers who, in their own ways, were trying to take the Muslim thought and culture in different directions and who have had such a profound impact on the rise and fall of Muslim civilisation.

Al-Ghazali's position is that only correct dogma can save believers, and philosophy and rational inquiry have no place in Islamic theology. His God is so omnipotent that He leaves no room for human agency; everything can be explained by miraculous intervention. Ibn Rushd argues that the Qur'an itself urges us to pursue rational deductions, to 'look into', 'consider' and 'reflect on' (2:29; 7:14) the wonders of creation as a means to understand God as Creator. Philosophy and science are thus central to all Islamic pursuits. If it turns out that rational inquiry was not conducted by Muslims but by the ancients (that is, the Greeks), then it is incumbent upon Muslims to embrace their thought and learning. Al-Ghazali argues that the Muslim 'community does not agree on error', therefore the consensus of the Muslim community (*ijma*) is binding on everyone. It is obligatory for every Muslim to follow the consensus; to differ from it is prohibited. Ibn Rushd, in contrast, argues that a human community can never reach a consensus with certainty on uncertain theological matter. To make it binding is to suggest that it is on par with the Qur'an and the traditions of the Prophet. In any case, he argues, there is more than one way to understand scripture. Al-Ghazali wants to instil fear of God and hell in his readers; Ibn Rushd argues that a society is free when no one acts out of fear of God or hell, or out of desire for reward in paradise, but for the love of God and humanity. Al-Ghazali freely uses hadith (authentic and weak, as well as quite irrational) and the sayings of sages and saints to make his arguments. Ibn Rushd unapologetically scrutinises the traditional sources with a critical and rational eye.

Both were jurists. In his legal text, Al-Ghazali denounces most allegorical interpretations as *kufr* (disbelief). Ibn Rushd, on the other hand, sees such literalism as anathema. Moreover, Al-Ghazali was a misogynist who compared women to ten kinds of animals, all of which except one, the sheep, were nasty. Ibn Rushd, on the other hand, believed that women were prescribed the same ultimate goals as men, that there is no question of men being superior to women. It is men who consider women as animals to be domesticated, or as plants which are sought for their fruit. These are traditions made by men to serve their own ends, and they have nothing to do with Islam.

The difference between the two scholars is also illustrated in Ibn Rushd's reply to Al-Ghazali in his *Incoherence of Incoherence*. There is no long preface throwing abuse and scorn at theologians in general or Al-Ghazali in particular. The book opens with a very brief and clear statement of purpose, which is to prove that *The Incoherence of the Philosophers* 'has not reached the degree of evidence and of truth'. Ibn Rushd refers to Al-Ghazali by name, and respectfully calls him Sheikh. Then it is down to business: Al-Ghazali's arguments are torn to shreds systematically and thoroughly in a series of sixteen 'discussions'.

First, Ibn Rushd argues that God's knowledge could not be categorised as 'universal' and 'specific' since these are human conceptions. God being God has a somewhat different perception of knowledge. We as humans are limited in our perception and cannot comprehend, much less categorise, Godly knowledge. Second, Ibn Rushd argues that human conduct is neither totally free nor fully determined – there is a third option: it is a bit of both. Humans have free will and are free to choose but the choice is also determined by external factors. Humans act to fulfil their hopes, desires and aspirations, which change over time. God, who is Eternal, simply acts as He is not bound by space and time. While defending allegorical interpretations of the Qur'an, Ibn Rushd suggests that not all methods of interpretation are equally valid. And he accuses Asharites of fanaticism for condemning philosophers as heretics and everyone else who does not agree with their theology. 'In truth, it is they who are the unbelievers and in error,' he says.

Incoherence of Incoherence[31] is a long, complex and

---

31 There are several translations of Ibn Rushd's *The Incoherence of the Incoherence* but the best is by Simon van Den Bergh, Luzac, London, 1954 (combined two volumes), which is the one I have used.

closely argued text – not easy to summarise. However, demolishing *The Incoherence of the Philosophers* was a relatively easy task for Ibn Rushd. A more challenging duty was critiquing other Mutazila philosophers, particularly Ibn Sina. Here, Ibn Rushd restores the agency to ordinary believers that both Al-Ghazali and Ibn Sina had denied. Once again, Ibn Rushd argues for the middle position between Al-Ghazali and Ibn Sina that allows for the doctrine of free will to exist without denying God's omniscience. He sees humanity as an active agent in Islam, and not a passive, predetermined one. Despite external constraints, individuals have the power to act, to shape their lives, to influence society and shape the future.

Ibn Rushd tries to bring philosophy and religion together in *On the Harmony of Religion and Philosophy*, written in a persuasive style for the educated public and from the point of view of a jurist. It explores whether philosophy and logic are permitted or prohibited by the Qur'an, the traditions of the Prophet, and Islamic law. Ibn Rushd argues that philosophy is nothing more than teleological study of the world. In as far as the Qur'an encourages a scientific, teleological study of the world, it encourages philosophy, which means reason and logic have to be amongst the tools required to study scripture and shape Islamic law. Revealed truths, he argues further, are true 'in the religious realm', and those of the world 'in the philosophic realm', but there is no contradiction between them: 'We the Muslim community know definitely that demonstrative study does not lead to conclusions conflicting with what scripture has given us.'[32] When apparent contradictions arise, it is the function of philosophy to reconcile the contradictions. For Ibn Rushd, the method for reconciling these apparent contradictions is allegorical and metaphorical interpretation of the Qur'an in such a manner that the inner meaning of Qur'anic verses are seen to agree with observed and demonstrative truth.

Ibn Rushd was a close friend of another Andalusian freethinker: Ibn Tufayl. He was born near Granada and served as chief physician to the Almohad Caliph Abu Yaqub Yusuf (reigned 1163–84). The caliph, a man of learning with a passion for philosophy, was an avid collector of books and also of learned men. His court was brimming with thinkers, writers and poets who openly argued and critiqued each other and the caliph. When Ibn Tufayl

32 Ibn Rushd, *On the Harmony of Religion and Philosophy*, op cit.

brought Ibn Rushd into the circle, the caliph immediately commissioned the philosopher to write a commentary on Aristotle. That commission, and the subsequent patronage by Abu Yaqub, as George Hourani notes in his introduction to *Averroes: On the Harmony of Religion and Philosophy*, had far-reaching consequences in the history of thought. It gave a new boost to philosophy in Islam and brought it to Jewish and Christian circles in Europe. It enabled Ibn Rushd not only to take on Al-Ghazali but also to reformulate Islamic philosophy.

Abu Yaqub's patronage also permitted Ibn Tufayl to write *Hayy ibn Yaqzan* ('Alive, Son of Awake'),[33] a philosophical novel of profound significance. The protagonist Hayy is spontaneously generated on an isolated desert island. He is adopted by a gazelle, learns survival skills, and after the death of his 'mother', on whom he performs an autopsy, sets out on the road to scientific and self-discovery. Through his observations and deductions, Hayy finally reaches the ultimate truths and realises that there is a Creator.

There are two significant points about *Hayy*. The first is

---

33 Simon Ockley's 1708 translation of *Hayy ibn Yaqzan* can be downloaded from: http://www.muslimphilosophy.com/books/hayy.pdf.

widely recognised: Ibn Tufayl argues that reason is a pow-
erful tool for understanding and shaping the world, and
offers us an evolutionary take both on humanity and on
human thought and development. The second is somewhat
neglected: Ibn Tufayl is more than aware of the limitations
of reason, despite Al-Ghazali's erroneous allegations. For
a major aim of the book is to show that reason alone is
not enough to experience the divine. Indeed, Ibn Tufayl
insists that even the conceptualisation of the divine is not
possible through reason and mundane experience. When
Hayy reaches the final stages of his philosophical journey, he realises that he cannot gain an understanding of
the supernatural by studying the material world. There
is also a jibe at Al-Ghazali here. The Baghdadi professor had identified the heart, in line with Sufi tradition,
as the part which is receptive to the divine unveilings,
the place where God is experienced. Ibn Tufayl dismisses
this notion. Rather, Ibn Tufayl suggests that the experience of the divine is spread across the human body; and
to describe this experience is misguided and impossible.
Our words just cannot do it justice. All attempts at such
description lead straight to the authoritative version: the
theology of orthodoxy, based on hearsay and superficial

constructions. Instead, Ibn Tufayl proposes an alternative: spiritual development is a journey that individuals take for themselves. Having brought the reader to a level of understanding of the world and purpose of life in which words no longer suffice, Ibn Tufayl declares: now you are on your own, the teacher can't help you, the Sheikh can only give you false directions. From here you have to take the next steps yourself to experience what I have experienced in my immersion in the divine. Once again, Al-Ghazali ends up looking rather lame.

The legacy of Ibn Tufayl and Ibn Rushd had a profound impact on Europe. It shaped the original Renaissance. Ibn Rushd produced a whole school of philosophy, Averroism; and his works became widely available at universities throughout Europe, and were responsible for the development of scholasticism, which examined Christian doctrines through the lens of reason and intellectual analysis. Indeed, he reached such a level of prominence in Europe that his translations were forbidden in thirteenth-century Paris, where he was accused of promoting freethinking. The 1671 Latin translation of *Hayy* under the title *The Self-Taught Philosopher* caused a sensation. It became the foundational text for British empiricism. John Locke's *An Essay*

Concerning Human Understanding was greatly influenced by *Hayy*; Locke's first draft of the *Essay* was completed in the same year his friend Edward Pococke finished and published the English translation of *Hayy*. It went on to influence a string of influential philosophers and writers, including Baruch Spinoza, Jean-Jacques Rousseau and Daniel Defoe.

In fact, it was not just Ibn Tufayl and Ibn Rushd that Europe embraced: it adopted the *adab* system in its totality. As the late George Makdisi, Professor of Arabic and Islamic Studies at University of Pennsylvania, who spent a lifetime studying how Islam humanised Europe, shows so painstakingly in *The Rise of Humanism in Classical Islam and Christian West*, there was hardly any aspect of Islamic humanism which Europe did not copy: from textbooks and academic institutions, structures and slogans to singularity in character, behaviour and dress; from emphasis on eloquence and display of literary prowess to the cult of classical language; from the works on government administration as part of moral philosophy to the history of cities, the novella, practical and speculative grammar to historical and textual criticism. Indeed, even the not-so-good traits of *adab* were adopted, thus reproducing some errors that are associated with Islamic humanism: the horror of barbarism and solecism.

The story in the Muslim world was somewhat different. The reasons for the evaporation of learning, philosophy and critical thought, and hence the decline of Muslim civilisations, are many and diverse. But there is little doubt that a major factor was the influence of Al-Ghazali. It was not the *Incoherence* itself, which is simply not a work of enough power to dethrone philosophy, and was probably read only by a select few. Rather, it was the aura built up around the book, within a context of an anti-philosophy hysteria whipped up by theologians, that did the most damage. Al-Ghazali became the epicentre of an anti-rationalist storm. He succeeded in resurrecting 'the sciences of religion', gave theology some respect and brought it back into the mainstream. But in the process his arrogant dismissal of reason, philosophy and forethought led to a downward spiral of Muslim civilisation.

The reduction of life

The theologians now had a spring in their step. First they closed 'the gates of *ijtihad*'. *Ijtihad*, which means 'sustained reasoning', is basically a shorthand for reason, criticism and rational thought in religious affairs. So by banning *ijtihad* they in fact outlawed all forms of critical reasoning in religious matters. This did not happen overnight; no committee of bearded scholars sat to make this decree. Rather, as Sadakat Kadri suggests in his *Heaven on Earth: A Journey Through Sharia Law*, it came to be treated 'as a historical fact rather than a poetically pleasing way of saying that jurists were no longer as good as they used to be'. Other category mistakes followed. Certain key Islamic concepts were similarly reduced in meaning. So, for example, *ilm*, the Qur'anic notion of knowledge, which had over 500 definitions and varieties during the classical period, was reduced from meaning all knowledge – including, most importantly, scientific knowledge – to simply meaning 'religious knowledge'. Al-Ghazali regarded *ijma*, consensus, in broad terms and talked about the consensus of the Muslim community. Indeed, he even included dead Muslims of the past as well as Muslims living in the present everywhere. But even the open-ended notion of Al-Ghazali's *ijma* was eventually reduced to mean only 'the consensus of religious scholars'. The rich notion of halal, which means permitted or praiseworthy, has social, cultural and environmental connotations and is a fundamental concept in Islamic ethics, was reduced to the level of halal meat. Slowly and gradually, life itself was reduced to one dimension, and Sunnism became narrower and narrower, more and more dogmatic and doctrinaire, and less and less tolerant of plurality and difference. Ultimately, it was drained of all ethical content. The *adab* tradition evaporated, leading to the disappearance of passion for knowledge and books as well as liberal humanism from Muslim cultures. The orthodoxy went further by banning music, art, theatre – anything that enhances our humanity – and drained Muslim civilisation of its rich culture. Sunni orthodoxy now consists of little more than manufactured dogma. The Shia, in contrast, did incorporate some aspect of Mutazila thought in their theology. Perhaps this is why Sunni fanatics are so aggressive towards the Shia community.

The true extent of Al-Ghazali's influence is well illustrated by C. Snouck Hurgronje, who, as the title of his book suggests, spent a considerable time in *Mekka in the Latter Part of the Nineteenth Century*. Hurgronje found that students in Mecca, who came from all over the world, were taught only the works of Al-Ghazali.

The Revival of the Religious Sciences was the main text; it was memorised by students by rote. Other texts 'were more or less excerpts or compilations from the works of Ghazali'. Not 'one new word' was to be heard anywhere. Philosophy was totally forbidden. 'The industrious students', Hurgronje writes, only understood that the philosophers 'were stupid pigheads who held human reason to be the measure of truth – a terrible superstition'. The professors openly mocked and ridiculed philosophers like Ibn Rushd, Ibn Tufayl and Ibn Sina: 'I have seen a smile of mocking astonishment pass over the faces of all students present when the professor told them how the ignorant heathens who opposed Muhammad, had, like the philosophers, believed in human reason, and the professor smiled too with a shrug of his shoulder.'[34] What was true of Mecca was true for the Muslim world as a whole.

To see where the theologians' revolt against reason and free thought has brought us, one need not look further than Saudi Arabia and Iran. Both the Sunni and Shia orthodoxies have been covered with layer upon layer of manufactured dogma that is as absurd as it is dangerously

---

34 C. Snouck Hurgronje, *Mekka in the Latter Part of the 19th Century*, translated by J. H. Monahan, Brill, Leiden, 2007, p. 210.

obsolete. Of course, the vast majority of orthodox Muslims, of both verities, are moderates and are truly horrified at what is being said and done in the name of Islam. But they have to realise that their cherished dogma, accepted so unquestioningly, has reduced them to dysfunctional societies and nations, and contains the seeds of strife and the horror they see all around their communities. The excesses of the extremists, non-violent and violent, are derived from the very dogma the moderates themselves believe to be true. Enough is enough. It is time to rethink what Islam means in the twenty-first century.

The rethinking must begin with sustained reasoning and free thought that cuts through dogmatism and takes us closer to God. It must be based on freedoms that the Mutazila fought so hard to protect: the freedom to reject the authorities of the past, including one's own teacher; the careful use of doubt as a means of searching for truth, including doubt about one's own position; and the freedom to choose an intermediate position between two extreme positions. It requires a return to the culture of *adab*, Islamic humanism, and love and compassion for all that the Mutazila championed.

Part III

The wound is the place
where light enters

A FEW YEARS AGO, I had dinner with a Muslim scientist. He is a leading expert on cancer cell biology and Professor of Neurology at a prominent American university. He had just published a paper that was seen as a major advance in cancer research, and, as a result, had been awarded a multi-million-dollar research grant. Congratulations were in order. We had a lively, and for me enlightening, discussion on his work.

He was engaging as well as self-critical about his research. Then the conversation moved, as it normally does amongst Muslims, to issues of religion. I noticed a recent publication on hadith on his bookshelf and commented on it. I said something like, 'It's about time we took a more reasoned and critical approach to hadith.' Suddenly his attitude changed. Scientific curiosity disappeared, critical thinking evaporated. Scratching his exceptionally fine Mahmal beard, he said, in a matter-of-fact way, there are no issues about hadith. Classical scholars have painstakingly sorted the authentic from the dubious. And it has been established beyond doubt, even by many Western scholars, that the canonical collections are perfectly reliable. To doubt hadith is to doubt Islam.

This is the power of orthodoxy in action. Over centuries, Islamic orthodoxy has shaped a mindset that turns the brain of even the most educated person into marshmallow. They can be highly critical in other spheres of life but when it comes to religion the critical faculties are suspended, conscience is put aside, and everything is accepted without question. They do as they are told by theologians and religious scholars, classical and contemporary, who have, by the grace of God, already solved all the problems of Islam and humanity. Given the attitude of highly educated people who would not hurt a proverbial fly, you can imagine how lesser minds with few scruples imbibe the orthodox traditions.

Ironically, the original approach to the sayings of the Prophet was based on critical judgement. When Bukhari and Muslim, the compilers of the two canonical collections, *Sahih al-Bukhari* and *Sahih Muslim*, set about their tasks there was no notion of criticism. So they invented a three-stage methodology of hadith criticism. First was the invention of *isnad* – the chain of narrators which had to be traced back to the Prophet. Second, each narrator in the chain had to be examined for faith, character, knowledge and the likelihood that he had actually met the people who preceded and succeeded him in the chain. The tradition had to be based on evidence as far as possible. And, finally, the hadith itself should not be contrary to the text of the Qur'an or reason.

Depending on how well the hadith fulfilled these criteria, it might be regarded as *sahih* or correct, *hasan* or a bit doubtful, or *daif* or weak. The weak hadith were then classified into a number of other categories such as those with missing chain of transmitters (*muallaq*), broken chain (*munqati*), fabricated (*maudi*) and so on. This was quite a sophisticated and critical methodology for the period. But the individuals who engaged in this erudite, meticulous, Herculean exercise were fallible human beings; and, as such, they were susceptible to human error. And errors there were; and they have haunted Islam ever since. One could ask, for example, why are so many authentic hadith clearly against reason when reason itself was one of the criteria for shifting authentic hadith from the false ones? Or, why do many hadith reflect the tribal obsessions, customs, concerns and misogyny of the time? Or, indeed, why do Sunnis, Shias and other sects use different sets of compilations, which are frequently contradictory? Why are so many hadith clearly designed to serve a political purpose? And was the methodology of hadith collection really so perfect that it cannot be questioned? Such questions are not tolerated by the orthodoxy simply because they undermine its own edifice.

Prisons of orthodoxy

Indeed, orthodoxy has incarcerated Islam in several prisons, each as confining as the others. The dubious use of hadith to silence all criticism and discussion is just one such penitentiary. Others include the literal interpretations of the Qur'an, Shariah, tradition, reverence and gullible acceptance of what the classical scholars say, the unquestioning authority of the so-called religious scholars and the madrassas, where the next generation is browbeaten into submission. These prisons are the root cause of the problems of all varieties of fundamentalism, literalism and extremism. The only real and lasting solution to extremism – from non-violent all the way to ISIS – is to break the walls of these prisons and free the intellect and the conscience of the believers.

The escape from Islamic orthodoxy begins with asking critical questions. These are the kinds of questions raised by the students of Belle Vue Girls' School and much earlier by the Mutazila and other freethinkers attempting to liberate Muslim thought. Many of these questions concern the fundamental sources of Islam. Regarding the Qur'an, for example, we need to ask: Is every injunction in the Sacred Text universal? What in the Qur'an is contextual and thus merely historical? Is it a text to be consumed or interrogated? What are we to do with the 'difficult' verses – the one, for example, that allegedly allows men to beat their wives? Does all morality and knowledge converge towards the Qur'an or diverge from it? Is classical interpretation, which knew nothing of modern linguistic, interpretative theory and hermeneutics, eternal? Why can't we undertake a philosophical critique of the Qur'an, which has been applied to the Bible and the Old Testament, without affecting their integrity? And what's wrong with ordinary Muslims interpreting the Qur'an for themselves?

Concerning hadith, we can ask: If the methodology of hadith compilation could allow irrational hadith into the corpus, what can we say about the authenticity of others? Are we to take everything we find in the canonical collections as absolute truths? A great deal is made of the meticulous way in which the compilers went about their business. There is, for example, the famous story of Imam Bukhari who is said to have travelled for miles to collect a hadith from a man. When he arrived at his house, he saw that the man was enticing his donkey with a bundle of hay. He returned without talking to the man, saying that a man who tricks his donkey is not a reliable witness. But what if he had arrived a few minutes earlier, or a few minutes later? It is said that he collected over 600,000 hadith, talking to over a thousand men, but only included 7,275 in his collection of authentic hadith. What happened to the rest? Did they remain in circulation? Moreover, should we be using hadith as a source of the Shariah – allegedly divine and eternal?

Beyond critical questioning, certain key suppositions of Islamic orthodoxy need to be dethroned. Perhaps the most important presumption is that the Shariah is divine. Almost any injustice on God's bountiful earth can be, and is or at one time or another has been, justified in the name of the Shariah: from apostasy, blasphemy, misogyny, xenophobia, inhuman punishments right down to totalitarianism. Ordinary Muslims – to be regarded as Muslims – must submit to the Shariah, or rather the interpretation of well-meaning religious scholars long dead and their cynical, manipulating and power hungry contemporary counterparts – composed as they are of a spectrum that runs all the way from those educated at prestigious institutions such as Al-Azhar University of Cairo, to the alumni of the fanatical and fundamentalist universities of Riyadh, Medina and Mecca in Saudi Arabia, to the myopic scholars of the Deoband seminary in India, right down to the semi-literate mullahs in the mosques of Britain. During the heyday of the Mutazila, the Shariah was a problem-solving methodology, aimed at solving ethical and practical issues of Muslim societies. But under the influence of orthodoxy it has evolved into a system that is morally timid but politically expedient, a system that renders Islamic reason indistinguishable from reason of state, and has degenerated into a morbid pathology. It has become self-authenticating and self-referential. An urgent task for enlightened Muslims is to reformulate the Shariah according to its ethical and social objectives (known as *maqasid*) based on the needs and requirements of our time.

Breaking out of prison

Of course, the orthodox religious scholars would argue that as a divine institution, Shariah cannot be changed. Fortunately, there are critical Muslims out there who not only argue that it can change but who have actually changed the Shariah. The most striking example is the new Islamic personal law in Morocco, known as the Moudawana.[35] It

---

35 The background story of how the Islamic law was changed is well told in 'Moudawana: a peaceful revolution for Moroccan women', at tavaana.org and by Anna Virkama, *Discussing Moudawana: Perspectives on Family Code Reform, Gender Equality and Social Change in Morocco*, Lambert Academic Publications, Saarbrucken, 2009. The English translation of the full text of the Moudawana can be downloaded from: http://www.hrea.org/programs/gender-equality-and-womens-empowerment/moudawana.

treats the Shariah not as divine but as a human construction, and introduces some revolutionary transformations with the explicit aim of establishing true gender equality. It throws out the centuries-old notion that the husband is the head of the family and the wife a mere underling in need of guidance and protection. Rather, it suggests that the Qur'anic notion of equality means that women are equal partners in marriage and family life. Moreover, the Moudawana regards women as independent, thinking beings and allows them to contract a marriage without the legal approval of a guardian. It also raises the minimum age for women's marriage from fifteen to eighteen, the same as for men. It consigns 'triple talaq' – where a man can divorce his wife by simply saying 'I divorce you' three times – to the dustbin of history. Outlawing verbal divorce, the Moudawana requires men to have prior authorisation from a court, and gives women equal rights to divorce – no questions asked. Moreover, under the Moudawana women can claim alimony and can be granted custody of their children even if they remarry. Husbands and wives must share property acquired during the marriage. The old custom of favouring male heirs in the sharing of inherited land has also been dropped, making it possible for grandchildren on the daughter's side to inherit from their grandfather, just like grandchildren on the son's side. While it apparently permits polygamy, in reality it all but abolishes it. The ambiguity here is a reflection of the ambiguity of the Qur'anic verse which gives permission to marry 'two, three or four' but 'if you fear that you cannot be equitable to them, then marry only one' (4:3). The Moudawana allows a man to take a second wife only with the full consent of the first wife and only if he can prove, in a court of law, that he can treat them both with absolute justice – an impossible condition. All these reforms, introduced in February 2004, are justified with verses from the Qur'an and examples from traditions of the Prophet Muhammad. And every change required and obtained the consent of the religious scholars, who, it must be noted, also included women. It is not surprising that even Islamist political organisations welcomed the change.

The prison of the Shariah exists within another prison – the 'Islamic state'. It is basically a state where the Shariah is supreme and the guardians of the Shariah, the religious scholars, are the rulers. The term itself is an oxymoron: Islam is a universal faith, a state is a parochial entity bound by geography, so how can you confine one into the other?

The common answer is by force. In post-revolutionary Iran, the Ayatollah Khomeini developed a system of governance where only those familiar and versed in the Shariah were deemed capable of creating and ruling a Muslim society. On top of an all-seeing and all-knowing Guardian of Jurists sits the infallible Supreme Leader. No one can stand for election, can say anything or do anything, without the explicit consent of the mullahs. In Saudi Arabia, the religious scholars, in cahoots with the royal family, enforce the Shariah with a stick and a sword. The obnoxious, semi-autonomous religious police, whose formal title is the Committee for the Propagation of Virtue and Prevention of Vice, function as an instrument of state repression. They ensure that believers stick to the narrow, monolithic Wahhabi notion of Islam. In these ideal Islamic states, freedom of expression is unknown, justice is arbitrary and politically expedient, and women are treated as dirt. In both Saudi Arabia and Iran, which Shariah-demanding fanatics in countries such as Pakistan, Bangladesh and Sudan wish to emulate, the prisons are full of dissidents, torture is routine, and legitimate opposition to government is seen as blasphemy. The 'Islamic State' of ISIS is the logical conclusion of this aberration.

Fortunately, there is a community that has rejected the notion of an Islamic state as not only untenable but intrinsically antithesis to the spirit of Islam. In 1998, just after the fall of Suharto, the dictator who ruled for three decades, Indonesia was faced with a choice. The ultra-conservative forces were demanding that the country should adopt the Shariah and become an Islamic state. The secularists naturally wanted a strongly secular state, where religion was confined to ritual and piety. But the two largest and most influential organisations in the country, Muhamadiyah and Nahdatul Ulama (NU), had other ideas. Conventionally NU, which is essentially an organisation of religious scholars, has been described as traditionalist, while Muhamadiyah, dominated by intellectuals and thinkers, was seen as modernist. Both were established at the dawn of the twentieth century, and together command sixty to eighty million followers spread across a vast network of mosques, schools and universities throughout Indonesia. Muhamadiyah and Nahdatul Ulama worked together to usher Indonesia towards an intermediate position they called 'deformalisation'. It had two 'missions'. First, to separate the Shariah from the political realms. In Saudi Arabia, Iran and Pakistan, Shariah is imposed from the above by the state. But these scholars and intellectuals argue that Shariah is a moral choice the citizens make for themselves and has to evolve from the grass roots to meet the demands of the twenty-first century. Second, Islam itself had to be 'deformalised'. 'Formalised Islam' – that is, Islam as conceived by conservative and radical groups and used as an instrument of state tyranny, with its emphasis on formality and symbolism – they argued, has drained Islam of its ethical and humane dimension. The goal of politics in Islam, they suggested, is to create a thriving civic society which returns Islam to the bosom of rich tradition of Islamic humanism. The result of these innovative reforms in Islamic thought was the pluralistic, thriving democracy that we now witness in Indonesia.[36] So, as Indonesia shows, the will of ordinary men and women can lead to a new and transformed understanding of the will of God!

But the hard-line religious scholars are not just the guardians of the Shariah and the Islamic state; they are also protectors of 'authentic Islamic tradition'. In essence, Muslim tradition is little more than medieval Arab tribal

---

36 Nadirsyah Hosen, *Shari'a and Constitutional Reform in Indonesia*, Institute of South Asian Studies, Singapore, 2007.

customs that have been enshrined in Islamic law and morality. In his *The Reconstruction of Religious Thought in Islam*, Muhammad Iqbal, the great visionary poet of the Indian subcontinent, called it 'Arabian imperialism of the earlier centuries of Islam'.[37] It is best exemplified in the widely believed dictum that 'religious scholars (the *ulama*) have solved all our problems' so now all the believers had to do is follow not only the interpretations of the classical authors, however absurd or out of date, but also their mode of thinking, which they have kindly perfected for future generations for all eternity. Several generations of Muslims who have grown up on the literature of the 'Islamic movement' – produced by Jamaat-e-Islami of Pakistan and the Muslim Brotherhood of Egypt – imbibe this tradition. And the vast majority of conservative Muslims, not aligned to the Islamic movement, including those who do not see themselves as Wahhabis, follow the tradition blindly – just like the Professor of Neurology I met a few years ago. For the traditionalist it provides ready-made solutions to everything without recourse to the mind, or to unnecessary concerns about justice, equality or even

---

37 Muhammad Iqbal, *The Reconstruction of Religious Thought in Islam*, Ashraf, Lahore, 1965, p. 134.

education. And when all else fails, violence can be used to enforce the traditionalist viewpoint. For critical Muslims, this tradition and dangerously obsolete mode of thought has now become a medieval torture chamber.

The institution where this traditional attitude is propagated is the madrassa. When the Mutazila thought was at its zenith, a madrassa was a place where you learned *adab*, critical thinking, logic, mathematics, astronomy, social sciences and humanities in addition to Islamic studies. But like much else, the madrassas are now reduced to the propagation of obscurantist tradition. Traditionalist madrassa education now relies exclusively on rote learning and incessant quoting of opinions of old theologians who ought to be left where they belong – in history. Reverence is the order of the day in a black-and-white universe where Islam is reduced to a monolithic set of rigid dos and don'ts that have little relevance to the contemporary world. The end product is a closed, unquestioning mind, kept on the straight and narrow by constant reference to hell and damnation – the kind of mentality that can easily be persuaded to engage in jihad as exemplified so well by the Taliban. In Britain, we have over 2,000 madrassas, which have some checks and balances regarding health and safety, but are not regulated in terms of *what* and *how* they teach. The closing of the Muslim mind is one of the greatest tragedies of modern history.

The madrassas, paralysed tradition, and religious scholars are bound together by the superglue of submission, reverence and a carefully calculated and cultivated veneration of authority. There is only one way I can think of to break the stranglehold of this three-headed fiend: free thought and merciless criticism in the style of the Mutazila. This is not an invitation to return to Islamic history. Rather, a summons to move forward with the spirit of questioning and criticism, reason and rational thought, the concern for justice and unity, the celebration of human society and pluralism, and the 'intermediate position' – which is essentially a notion of doubt and compromise – that the Mutazila believed Islam was all about. It is, of course, a long-term and multi-generational undertaking. And it is largely a task for the Muslim community itself.

But it is also a task that can begin immediately here in Britain. For example, the curriculum of the madrassas can be regulated a bit more thoroughly to ensure that they concentrate less on memory and more on critical understanding of Muslim faith. Here, the madrassas can

take a leaf from the teaching methods of Belle Vue Girls'
School and incorporate 'philosophy for children' in their
curriculum, and encourage their students to read the texts
of different sects, and ask questions that are based on
thought and reflection. This is something the madrassas are not designed to do, so they have to be persuaded
through legislation and inspection. Similarly, we need to
introduce serious reforms in British mosques. Most of
the mosques in Britain are managed and run by narrow-
minded Deobandis who have turned them into enclaves
of ultra-conservatism. They may not be breeding extremists – who acquire their ideology from the internet – but
they do promote misogyny, cerebral atrophy on issues of
religion, and dislike – if not downright hatred – of other
sects and faiths. The trustees of these mosques suppose
to reflect the rich diversity of British Muslim life. But
in reality almost every mosque has bearded men from a
single sect as self-appointed trustees who are not willing
to change. Moreover, most imams, including those apparently 'trained in Britain', are insular and reactionary if not
semi-literate. Clearly, there needs to be a wide-ranging
review of the management of British mosques, appropriate training of imams with open minds and ability to

discuss and persuade, and strict guidelines on how imams are appointed. Then there are the so-called religious scholars. At the moment, almost anyone, literate, semi-literate or totally ignorant, can describe themselves as an *alim*, or religious scholar. All they need to set up shop – start giving advice and fatwas in a mosque or on YouTube, teaching in a madrassa, or preaching on an evangelical channel – is to be able to quote a few verses of the Qur'an and a handful of hadith by memory. Contrast this with the rabbis or priests who have to study for years and go through long, arduous training. However, there are some religious officials who are trained in the universities of Saudi Arabia, the seminaries of Deoband, or similar traditionalist institutions. Sometimes these folks are specially imported to propagate blinkered ultra-conservatism. More often, they arrive in our living rooms through numerous Islamic television channels and YouTube videos. (Here's some homework for you: zap the Islamic channels on your Sky/Virgin box and see how many terrifying beards and burqas you can identify.) A good example is Farhat Hashmi, a *niqabi* Pakistani Wahhabi female mullah based in Canada, who thinks it is a wife's absolute duty to obey her husband no matter how oppressive, violent and beastly he may be. Her obnoxious

YouTube sermons are part of the standard religious diet in many traditional British Muslim households. These are precisely the type of 'scholars' we don't need in Britain. We desperately need scholars educated in British universities, preferably with a postgraduate qualification, with a degree of critical acumen. Again, the British Muslim communities, conservative by nature and traditionalist by outlook, are not going to move willingly in this direction and have to be sturdily nudged.

There are segments of the Muslim community that do appreciate the importance of criticism and free thought in religious matters and are doing their best to encourage it. The Inclusive Mosque Project, for example, involves numerous young people who have been working for some years to 'create an inclusive sacred space that welcomes people of all ages, race, ability, sexual orientation, gender, ethnicity, culture, language, social status, education and religion'. The Muslim Institute, 'a palace that exists to promote and support the growth of thought, knowledge, research, creativity and open debate', specifically aims to revive the great tradition of the Mutazila criticism and free thought. The kind of critical questions I have raised are openly discussed at the Institute's meetings and conferences. The Institute's innovative publication, *Critical Muslim*, published quarterly as a paperback book, aims 'to seek new readings of religion and culture with the potential of social, cultural and political transformation of the Muslim world'.

There is also awareness of the fact that we need new and critical methods of teaching Islam. The International Forum for Islamic Dialogue (IFID), which is largely a Shia network, aims to build critical capacity of young Muslims, and equip them intellectually and practically to engage with the complex problems of Muslim societies. IFID has developed a ground-breaking method of teaching Islam that encourages young Muslims to engage critically with the fundamental sources of Islam – the Qur'an, hadith and classical texts. Every year, hundreds of young students and scholars attend its workshops, seminars and conferences. The International Institute of Islamic Thought (IIIT) has undertaken a more ambitious venture to reform education throughout the Muslim world. It recognises that the problem is not just in how Islam is perceived and taught, but also the teachings of science, engineering and medical subjects as well as the acute lack of social sciences in Muslim countries. The overall goal of IIIT's 'Educational

Reform' project is 'integration of knowledge', and the development of an educational system that emphasises critical thinking, promotes the great tradition of Islamic humanism, and aims to shape more rounded moderate and analytical minds.

So the Muslim community is by no means passive. The more enlightened members of the community are actively trying to rediscover the rich and diverse history of critical thought and humanism in Islam. Our community does not lack intellectual resources: we have some of the best Muslim intellectuals, thinkers, academics and writers in the world. To dethrone the edifice of Islamic orthodoxy, to reinvent tradition as a critical enterprise, to reinterpret Islamic sources in new and innovative ways, to reformulate the Shariah, to introduce rational thought and questioning in madrassas and religious education, to make our mosques more diverse and accountable – these are formidable tasks. But they can become even more arduous in an atmosphere of Islamophobia and hostility towards the Muslim community.

And quite impossible when the enlightened segments of the Muslim community are caught in a pincer movement. From one side, the extremist elements constantly attack, dismiss and declare critical and freethinking individuals and groups as 'bad Muslims' and 'heretics'. Email, Twitter and other social media make it easy to abuse and threaten them, and thus sap their efforts and energy. From the other side, Britain's foreign policy provides fuel and swells the numbers of the very extremists that freethinkers are trying to counter and contain. Britain props up dictators when it suits and dislodges them when needed. Muslims in the Middle East, Afghanistan and Pakistan have been bombed constantly, with direct or indirect support of Britain, for the past two decades. When it comes to killing there is not much distinction between 'terrorists' and 'civilians'. The lies and euphemisms used to justify our foreign policy and its consequences only add insult to injury. Britain's relationship with Saudi Arabia is perhaps the best example of our hypocrisy and the nefarious nature of our foreign policy.

The monster's hive

Think of Saudi Arabia as the hive of the predator, the eponymous antagonist of the *Alien* movies. In the second instalment, *Aliens*, our heroine, Ripley, and the young girl she is protecting, Newt, walk into the egg chamber of the alien queen. It is simply the most frightening scene in the film. The egg chamber is Saudi Arabia, where fanatic Wahhabis and Salafis predators are being produced at the same speed that the alien queen spouts her eggs – a reality that I find just as frightening. We are justly horrified at the executions and brutality shown by ISIS, yet have remained silent at the executions, torture, floggings and other inhuman deeds that have been going on in Saudi Arabia for decades. In the kingdom, atrocity after atrocity, the results of greed and extreme behaviour, including the death of innocent pilgrims to Mecca, is dismissed as 'the will of God'. It is a place where you can be crucified for questioning the Shariah or asking a critical question about Islam. The Saudi blogger and editor of a liberal website, Raif Badawi, was sentenced to jail for ten years and sentenced to 1,000 lashes for 'violating Islamic values and propagating liberal thought'. During 2014/15, according to Amnesty International, the Saudi government

severely restricted freedoms of expression, association and assembly, and cracked down on dissent, arresting and imprisoning critics, including human rights defenders. Many received unfair trials before courts that failed to respect due process, including a special anti-terrorism court that handed down death sentences. New legislation effectively equated criticism of the government and other peaceful activities with terrorism. The authorities clamped down on online activism and intimidated activists and family members who reported human rights violations. Discrimination against the Shi'a minority remained entrenched; some Shi'a activists were sentenced to death and scores received lengthy prison terms. Torture of detainees was reportedly common; courts convicted defendants on the basis of torture-tainted 'confessions' and sentenced others to flogging. Women faced discrimination in law and practice, and were inadequately protected against sexual and other violence despite a new law criminalising domestic violence. The authorities detained and summarily expelled thousands of foreign migrants, returning some to countries where they were at risk of serious human rights abuses. The authorities made extensive use of the death penalty and carried out dozens of public executions.[38]

Yet Britain actively and successfully campaigned for, and

---

38 Amnesty International Report 2014/14, The State of the World's Human Rights, London, 2015, p. 313.

then welcomed the UN decision to appoint Saudi Arabia as chair of the United Nations Human Rights Council.

In this most inhuman of all human states, clerics issue fatwas on a daily basis justifying oppression of women; slavery; hatred of the Shia, Christians, Jews and all others; declaring evolution is unbelief and the earth is flat. Even a fatwa justifying paedophilia as 'God's Law' has been issued recently. It came from one of the highest religious authorities in the kingdom, Sheikh Salih bin Fawzan, a member of Saudi Arabia's Permanent Committee for Islamic Research and Fataawa, and was published in Saudi newspapers on 13 July 2011. Fawzan declared that 'uninformed interference with Sharia rulings by the press and journalists is on the increase, posing dire consequences for society, including their interference with the question of marriage to small girls who have not reached maturity, and their demand that a minimum age be set for girls to marry'. There is no minimum age, Fawzan said. The religious scholars – the *ulama* – 'have agreed that it is permissible for fathers to marry off their small daughters, even if they are in the cradle'. As is usual in such edicts, Fawzan quotes from the Qur'an and the traditions of the Prophet to justify his ruling. And he warns:

It behoves those who call for setting a minimum age for marriage to fear Allah and not contradict his Shariah, or try to legislate things Allah did not permit. For laws are Allah's province; and legislation is his exclusive right, to be shared by none other. And among these are the rules governing marriage.

Allah has also legislated, according to an earlier fatwa by Fawzan, that slavery is an integral part of Islam; and the Sheikh wants it re-introduced in Muslim societies. Now, more mature minds may dismiss this but this radical evil has a direct impact on Shariah-obsessed, ultra-conservatives in Britain. They are not only convinced of the truth of such fatwas but also attack, harass and label as 'heretics' those Muslims who are appalled by such edicts. Yet Britain is totally in thrall to the kingdom. We lower our flag when a Saudi king dies and our royalty and politicians rush to support the monarchy at every opportunity. And we are happy to sell them as many weapons as the clerics and royal family may need to suppress their own liberal folks and cause as much havoc in the world as possible. It seems, as Andrew Mitchell, the former Secretary of State for International Development, points out, that we have outsourced our foreign policy to Saudi Arabia.[39] Worse: we are happy for these clerics to come and take over our mosques, send their imams, and other preachers (they call them *dais*) to brainwash the Muslim community and its future generations.

How then can those struggling to reform Islam from within and promote questioning and critical free thought make headway?

Yet, the heretics are determined to take centre stage. Or, as Rumi put it, 'the wound is the place where light enters'. The light of dissent from a bankrupt and inhuman Islamic orthodoxy, both Sunni and Shia, is spreading both in Britain and in every country where Muslim communities are to be found. There is simply no other way to break out of the maze of prisons that the orthodoxy has created.

---

39 Andrew Mitchell, 'We've outsourced foreign policy to Saudi Arabia', *The Guardian*, 8 October 2015.

Last words

DURING MY YOUTH, I was a Muslim activist. I established an Islamic society at my school, ran the London Islamic Circle that met on Saturdays at the Central London Mosque Regent's Park, and became the General Secretary of the Federation of Student Islamic Societies (FOSIS) during my university years. So most of my youth was spent in gatherings of what we lovingly called 'brothers and sisters in Islam'. The most notable thing about my circle of friends was the absence of beards. An occasional individual would support a sprightly beard; but beards were an exception rather than the rule. Some 'sisters' covered their heads; but most did not. And we never heard the word *niqab*, let alone saw a woman wearing one. There were idealists, romantics and even puritans amongst us; and we argued, we debated, and we had the most ferocious intellectual battles – about the plight of the Muslim people, about education reform, about returning Islam to the glories of the past. But no one ever used the words 'Salafi', 'Wahhabi' or 'jihadi'. Indeed, I did not even know whether my closest friends were Sunni or Shia. All that mattered was that we were all working together to usher some sort of intellectual, social and political resurgence in Islam.

Those innocent ideals have now evaporated. Somewhere along the highway, history took several wrong turns. The changes in my own life are punctuated by these turns. The Iranian Revolution in 1979 brought out the sectarian divisions in Muslim societies. For the first time I became aware that one of my closest friends was a Shia. Ten years later, the Rushdie affair brought the puritans to the fore; and I discovered that a handful of my close companions were ever ready to be offended and outraged. I lost many of them when I refused to endorse the fatwa of Ayatollah Khomeini, as I believed then, and still do, that books should fight books – just as they have done in Islamic history. Then, by the turn of the millennium, when it became clear that a large number of mosques in Britain had been taken over by the Wahhabis and their cousins, the Deobandis, I began to be seen as not quite a 'proper Muslim'. Even the semi-literate imam at my local mosque tried to correct the way I (always) prayed. The Friday sermons became more and more fanatical and intolerant, and I concluded that my salvation, and the preservation of sanity, depended on avoiding the mosque altogether. At a talk I was invited to give at the Oxford University Islamic Society about the same time, I discovered that FOSIS, which shaped my activism and outlook during my youth, had been taken over by Wahhabi and Deobandi beards. I did not encounter a single student with an open mind. Truly, I thought, we are now shrouded in darkness.

Things have gone downhill ever since. I have watched in agony the horrors of 9/11, 7/7, Madrid, Mumbai, *Charlie Hebdo* and the Paris attacks unfold before my eyes. And I have cried endlessly at the slicing of Iraq, the annihilation of Afghanistan, the drone killings in Pakistan, the destruction of the Arab world – the 'war on terror' that terrifies me and has produced nothing but more terror. In the 1990s, we had al-Qaida and the Taliban; now we have a whole array of even more frightening and blood-thirsty mutations of the Taliban in Pakistan, as well as Boko Haram in Nigeria and al-Shabab in Somalia, and the most terrifying beast of all – ISIS.

The answer to this spiral of never-ending violence is not more violence. It may be necessary, in the short term, to defeat ISIS, and disarm and neutralise jihadi groups of all ilk. But this is not a permanent solution: we can't bomb people who claim to love death more than life into submission. The only viable alternative is to create an environment and culture where life can be sustained, where people are free of despotism and oppression, so life can be valued and living for God manifests itself as the true road to salvation. This cannot be done when for the sake of business we prop up vile and oppressive regimes in the Muslim world, selling them weapons of death and instruments of torture they use freely on their citizens. It cannot be done with a foreign policy that tends to resolve everything by bombing people, where only 'our security' matters but the security of others, and their suffering, is irrelevant, and viewed from a safe distance on television.

We cannot, on the one hand, denounce the fanatics, and on the other hand, sustain and nourish the regimes that produce fanaticism in the first place. If Britain's foreign policy continues to be dictated from Riyadh, then we should not be surprised that the fanatical jihadis continue to grow geometrically.

The Muslims themselves have a clear task: to rethink Islam, root and branch. Islam does not need a 'reformation' and a thirty-year religious war. We have already had that. Islam needs reformulation: it needs to ditch its manufactured, dangerously obsolete and divisive dogma, reformulate the Shariah, reconsider its relationship with politics, and rethink itself anew. It will take several generations. But it is a task that Muslims cannot avoid.

Which brings me back to my session with the students at Belle Vue Girls' School in Bradford. They reminded me of my own youthful idealism, which was mixed with religious euphoria; and it vaporised soon after the Iranian Revolution. But the Belle Vue sixth formers restored my idealism about the possibility of a reformulated Islam. They were not euphoric but pragmatic; and, more importantly, had the ability to use Islam's own system of critical thought and action to rethink Islam in pragmatic ways. But the

Belle Vue sixth formers are not unusual. In my travels in Britain and around the Muslim world I have encountered numerous people – mostly young, mostly women – who ask questions that pious, conservative Muslims never ask, indeed cannot ask. These questioning young people are what the Mutazila called advocates of 'autonomous reflection'. They are determined to break out of the fatal and fatalistic prisons of Wahhabi and ultra-conservative thought. And they know that power is never given but is always taken. Slowly, they are beginning to take power, to think for themselves, and surely they will transform the rotten centre of Islam from the periphery.

I am counting on that.